CU00840983

PEAKS TO THE POLE

Al Sylvester MBE

Printed in England

Copyright Al Sylvester MBE

First published in 2018

CONTENTS

FOREWORD

Al and I met through a mutual friend and work colleague, the late Dean Singleton. Al had recently returned from his holiday with his son Kieran as this tanned, mature and smiling man. I still recall his posture with crossed legs on the carpet of the living room beaming from ear to ear. His image at that time still deeply planted in my memory. This day was a new beginning for the both of us and we have travelled together on a path which I believe has been mapped out for us by destiny. Before I met Al, I had lived in Greece for many years and had lived my own eventful life. I had an interest in explorers and travel. I had the opportunity to read Endurance Shackleton's Incredible Voyage long before I met my future husband. Little did I know the man I met on 13 August 2004 was to travel to Antarctica and lead the Royal Air Force first unsupported expedition to the South Pole and become my husband. Within the early days of meeting Al and getting to know him it became apparent he was already in the early stages of preparing for an expedition. It would take two years in the time I had known him to come to fruition. The two years that followed, Al was a man without limits in determination, energy, enthusiasm and expectation, this has never left him! The two years that followed were somewhat a distant memory now on reflection as the years that came to be on his return from the South Pole were unimaginable in many ways. Having read and digested Shackleton's exploration of Antarctic I was somewhat prepared mentally for Al to return a changed man. What man could travel to the end of the earth, endure what Shackleton had and return unscathed. My fears were justified but not fully in the expectations I had mapped out in my mind but ways you will read and understand through the honesty this book will deliver. The harshness, the reality, the pain and tears that were bestowed on this man, who to so many perceived to be invincible in many ways. Through these pages you will encounter the expedition from the comfort of your position and travel the journey from the Peaks to the Pole. Will his days of challenge end at the conclusion of this adventure or will he strive to overcome personal defeat and be empowered further on this path we call life?

I am proud to be his wife and the mother of his son. But am I ready for this man to become transparent in his make-up and share with you what has become the reality for us? We would be selfish to keep the trials and tribulations to ourselves when so much is to be gained by truth and honesty. I have shared this man with his personal challenges, what would be gained by limiting him to them and not supporting him with this journal. Our adventures of life continue and so this narrative will give you an insight into the man known to many as Al Sylvester MBE.

Clare and Joshua Sylvester-Wyness

Chapter 1
CONCEPTION

So there I was sat at my desk at RAF Kinloss, sitting a gasp in disbelief that after being invited by the RAF Mountain Rescue Service (MRS) Mount Everest Expedition leader to apply for the expedition of a lifetime only 3 weeks ago, he was now informing me that he couldn't authorise both RAF Leuchars and Kinloss team leaders to both leave their positions for 3 months. I knew that the Leuchars team leader, Flight Sergeant Dan Carroll with 8000 metres experience should undoubtedly be the one to go, but this didn't help my punctured feelings having been told you're no longer invited. It wasn't just the deflating news, but the heartache it had caused as a married guy with children to actually come to my decision to commit to such a potentially life changing expedition. I knew deep down that the expedition leader had made the right choice but that phone call stuck in my throat for many months, only to be partially cleared by the news that Dan and Corporal Rusty Bale summited Everest on 21 May 2001, a date that l and many others treasure as one of the greatest days in RAF MRS history.

Life had moved on since 2001, with my retirement from RAF Kinloss MRS, including an 18 month posting down to the Defence Logistics Organisation at Andover, which saw my wife leave me and take away my son Kieran up to Beauly just North of Inverness. It was ironic when she broke the news to me, that she was moving to Beauly, as I replied that at least I could take him to the famous car museum. With the strangest of looks, she replied, *"there isn't a car museum there..."* I think the saying *"Never presume, always check"* comes to mind. Hey, in my defence don't Beauly and Beaulieu sound the same?

Over the next 6 months, I drove the 1150 mile round trip each fortnight to prove that although the ex wife could put a mountain or 2 in between Kieran and I, it wouldn't stop me seeing him, the lengths some people will go to hey! Simultaneously, while busting my backside between working and driving up the length of the country, I called in a few favours to arrange a posting back to RAF Kinloss within the Aeronautical Rescue Co-ordination Centre. As an MRS team leader this is an awesome posting as an assistant controller, as the centre provides search and rescue cover for the whole of the United Kingdom, both on land and at sea. The only negative aspect was that I had to live in the Warrant Officer's and Sergeants mess, which was not the best location for Kieran to stay with me; although I must say the staff were very helpful. This is where; having previously owned 2 houses in Scotland helped my plight. As my finances had been disappointingly shared with the ex, I didn't have the excess money to purchase a house. Although houses may have been on the market at a sensible £100K for a 3 bedroomed property, to outbid any other interested party, you needed at least £30K cash above the asking price to be in with a chance. So what do you do? Simple, you buy a brand new house and pay the builder the asking price. This is what I did and 3 months later Kieran and I moved into our new humble abode in Nairn. So there I was, in one of the best jobs in the RAF, settled down again, living in my own house with Kieran staying with me regularly and within an hour of the mountains.

It was early into an evening shift when Corporal Iain Kirk, a young RAF Police Officer (RAFP) came into the ARCC for a brew and to catch up on any rescues going on around the bazaars. The MRS troops regularly popped into the ARCC, as it was a great way of getting to know the various controllers and assistants for when the team were out on a rescue. Being able to read Kirky like a book was something that l had learnt as his team leader a few years before, as l could see he was brewing on telling me something. It only took 2 sips of his tea to tell me his account about how the senior RAF Policeman, the Provost Marshall, had put out his latest quarterly bulletin, encouraging RAFP and RAF Regiment to go out and fine some original way of promoting the security forces of the RAF. My interpretation of the Provost Marshall's message was, he wanted a way to prove that RAFP were not just there to arrest you while having fun and that the RAF Regiment, were not just there to teach you how to fire a weapon and annually gas you. Looking slightly nervous and apprehensive as to why he was telling me this, he innocently but very enthusiastically went on to tell me how he thought "WE" could organise an unsupported expedition to the South Pole… Well, how do you respond to such a request? Kirky, had obviously thought about this for a few hours, as his ideas were ricocheting around the ARCC like an adrenalin fueled junky.

My very first thoughts were of the immense size of organisation required to put an expedition of this scale together and then like a flash of inspiration, it hit me, this could be the major trip of a lifetime for me to organise and to replace my disappointment of not going to Everest. As Kirky left, l could see he walked out with a spring in his step, not realising that he had just fed me a lead weight of work with a hidden golden carrot.

Over the next couple of months, I made lots of enquiries with troops whom had organised big expeditions in the past to see what I was letting myself in for. I did this without passing on my intentions, as it soon became apparent, there had been several attempts over the past decade to organise an expedition to Antarctica, all of which had been unsuccessful, due to being unable to raise sufficient funds.

What also became transparent, this was going to be ground breaking territory in the Armed Forces adventurous training world, as to date, there had been no attempt made on the Geographic South Pole by any military team. You may question my last sentence, but Captain Robert Falcon Scott, Lieutenant Ernest Shackleton and Major Vivian Fuchs all ascended onto Antarctica as primarily scientific expeditions.

As the weeks passed the momentum in my head and the file of information started to build, with an element of belief that this adventure could actually happen. Then, a bomb shell: on what should have been one of the happiest days of my uncommission RAF career, I was told that I was being promoted to Warrant Officer as of 12 July 2004 with a posting to RAF High Wycombe, 35 miles outside London! What a dilemma. I'm working within one of the best jobs in the RAF, I have just rebuilt my life and home and most importantly I'm seeing Kieran on a regular basis. Over the next couple of weeks I weighed up all my options with the help of the guy in charge of the ARCC, Squadron Leader Nick Barr MBE. Thankfully Nick helped me look at the wider picture, of pensions, quality of life and the potential of a posting back up to Kinloss in 18 months. Additionally, there was the other side of the coin. RAF High Wycombe is home to Headquarters Strike Command, hosting the RAF's Senior Leadership Team, some of which had been in my chain in command during my years in mountain rescue. What immediately came to mind was the potential of a few doors opening towards financial support and guidance of how to project the expedition forward, as a result of the potential support of a few of the senior executive officers.

My new job at High Wycombe was back in my original trade of communications, working within Cryptographic Communications Security (COMSEC). I was about to embark on a vertical learning curve of literature to cram in before going live on the road making policy decision for troops who have been born and breathing this stuff since time began. Fortunately the teams of guys already in post were outstanding tradesmen, legends within the trade, all of who welcomed me with open arms and basically kept the transmission on until l had learnt enough to get me on the road. This initial month was a marker in the sand of the incredible level of support the team gave me throughout the whole of my journey.

It was obvious that as my primary duty involved working away visiting RAF units it was going to calm the progress but not my enthusiasm of organising the trip. On the flipside of the coin, the time away gave me the space I needed to evolve a solid foundation for the expedition. I had learned from my research and previous experience, that organising a trip of this scale needed to be built upon slowly, giving all the agencies involved time to consider the best way forward. As the itinerary of COMSEC reviews was laid out throughout the year, I could see the windows of opportunities for me to arrange interviews with the heads of sheds of RAF finance, catering, medical, dental, adventurous training, transport, equipment and of course the senior leadership. As each interview passed, what became apparent was each head of shed did not really care about the other areas as long as it didn't affect them. From my perspective, it felt like I was an architect, building a house. Each area required a specific size room, some larger than others, some required connecting doors and some needed padded walls. As the months and interviews passed, I built the ground floor, filling each room with contacts and procedures. This had taken 10 months but with the knowledge I had consumed I felt so much more confident that I could now put a ceiling on each room and start climbing the stairs to build the first floor. The first floor only had 3 rooms, 1 for the RAF's Commander in Chief, 1 for Antarctic Logistics Expeditions (ALE) leaving the final room for me.

ALE is a civilian company, one of only 2 franchises who could fly my team onto Antarctica and provide us verbal support during our time on the ice. And as we were flying from Chile, this was the company for us. ALE would also be the recipient of at least £124K of the money required to proceed with our attempt; hence having a first floor room.

I had known the RAF's Commander In Chief Sir Brian Burridge for many years as he had been my Station Commander at RAF Kinloss in the 90's, my Air Officer in Command of mountain rescue in 2000 and was now the second in command of the whole of the RAF in 2004. As Sir Brian was extremely busy, appointments were rigidly tight and as for being a Warrant Officer getting the opportunity, to meet up with him, made me a little nervous. On arrival of his office, I immediately announced my intentions and how an expedition to Antarctica could put the RAF ahead of game in comparison to the Army and Royal Navy. Sir Brian became increasingly more interested and inquisitive which led me nicely into asking him to consider being the expedition's military patron. His immediate positive response was soon engulfed with a mandatory clause of a guarantee that I must bring all 4 members back in one piece. With farewell handshakes completed, l floated out of his history filled office, thinking for the first time in 9 months, this trip may actually go ahead. It was only when I returned to the COMSEC team that I realised that my 20 minute meeting had actually taken 40, Sir Brian was definitely on board.

The timing of the interview with Sir Brian was perfect in regards to Kirky, who for the past four months had been serving on Operation Telic, where he worked in the war zone of Basra, Iraq. While out there, even in the 40 plus degrees heat, Kirky had been spending every spare hour training and building up his stamina.

June 05
After speaking to Kirky and passing on the great news, we now had the credibility to set about recruiting a South Pole team. The military has a

network of communications established to advertise expeditions, so with minimum details exposed, as I didn't want to blow this trip out of the water before we had even taken a step forward, we advertised the expedition around all RAF stations. After 2 weeks we had only received 1 reply from a troop whose name will remain anonymous throughout this book as I have not gained his permission to print his actual name, so the for purposes of this book he will be referred to as Pita. Pita quickly came on board with ideas of how to take the expedition forward. But with only 1 volunteer, we needed to expand our advertisement with a greater description and to a wider audience. Together, we reworded the advert, this time receiving 31 replies from varying ranks, ages, sex and trade. Included within the replies was a lady from the Royal Navy, but as l was determined to maintain this as an RAF expedition only. With copies of everyone's CV in front of Kirky, Pita and I we scrutinized each person, reducing our list down to 18 possibilities. Any candidate that we didn't approve, I spoke to them on the phone. As I'd never embarked on a task of this nature, I wanted to ensure that the credibility of the expedition should be maintained whether presenting good or bad news.

We then geographically split the candidates between the 3 of us to allow everyone a fair attempt at promoting themselves to the expedition. A standard set of questions were set to be posed to each person, so that an overall evaluation could be made, without any bias.

To help me with the interview, I asked 2 of my friends to assist me, an occupational psychologist and a junior officer, with no mountaineering experience to gain their opinions of the candidates. My 5 candidates all arrived punctually and impeccably dressed for the interview, endorsing their seriousness of intent. Of all the candidates who l met over that 3 day period, one troop, Corporal Phil Mainprize really impressed me not only with his level of skiing experience but also his enthusiasm and overall likeability of his character. Additionally unbeknown to Phil, I had received a letter from his boss at RAF Halton, emphasising what an all round top troop he was. Although this didn't sway my decision, I must admit everything that his boss had written, certainly came out in the interview. The interview phase left me with 10 troops, including Kirky and Pita. After experiencing the difficult calls of phoning the unsuccessful candidates, l thoroughly enjoyed passing on the good news to my team who now knew they were all 1 step closer to stepping on the ice of Antarctica.

The most important factor now was to bring all the chosen guys together as a team and to put forward a plan of how to raise around £180K over the next 18 months. So in pencil I put together a rough itinerary of training weekends in the UK and 2 training expeditions to Iceland, with a final assessment trip to Norway. What was ironic was that the itinerary I put together overlapped a week's leave that I'd booked to go on holiday, which meant as expedition leader, I actually missed the first training weekend.

The reason as to why my leave was so important was for the following reason. My great friend Dean Singleton who I'd had served within the MRS at both Kinloss and Stafford was now a police officer in Wiltshire working out of the main station in Highworth, near Swindon. As I was spending hour after hour in the evening researching Antarctica, Dean invited me to his house as he was having a party with a few work colleagues. Keeping to tradition with previous MRS parties, I arrived early with 24 cans of beer and a bottle of whisky. With a wry smile, Dean welcomed me in and we shared a few cheeky beers before the first knock on the door. Stood at the door was a gorgeous lady with long dark hair, who I invited into Dean's humble abode. As the lady named Clare and I approached the kitchen, Dean broke the news that the evening was actually a blind date for the 2 of us and that curry was on the menu with wine and my beer. This was a typical Dean stunt, whose smile and perfect execution of planning was impeccable. We all enjoyed a wonderful evening, although Clare who was on duty the next morning, remained sober, while Dean and I sank several bottles of wine. Our relationship blossomed over the coming months, resulting in Clare inviting me over to her apartment in Crete, hence missing the first training weekend.

July 05
During the weekend meet, the troops got to know each other, various tasks were delegated and a pencil plan was worked on to start raising this immense amount of cash. What happened over the next couple of weeks was something as a military expedition I should have predicted to happen. 2 troops were forced to withdraw, as 1 of their bosses had recognised early into the proceedings that

he could not release his troop for such a length of time to complete all the training and then the main expedition itself, in fact, he was to be detached to Afghanistan within the next 2 months for an indefinite period of time. The other troop had followed my instructions to have a stringent medical to ensure there were no hidden problems that I needed to know about prior to starting this onslaught of intense training. Unfortunately, he had many years previously encountered problems with one of his kidneys, so any form of dehydration was a none starter, so within 2 weeks I had lost a fifth of my team.

I delegated Squadron Leader Kev Eaton from RAF Cranwell as the financial coordinator, which allowed me space and time to crack on organising the team's first overseas skiing training expedition. As with every military expedition, the rain forest equivalent of paperwork required to just establish the trip was a challenge within itself, bearing in mind the Commanding authority aspect of Headquarters Strike Command were still pondering on the feasibility of the main South Pole expedition coming off at all. Considering the time of year, i.e. November, the location had to achieve all our training needs and be of the minimum cost. The idea of Iceland came to me, as the RAF MRS use to participate in joint exercises with the United States Air Force (USAF) Parachute rescue teams across on the glaciers in the early 1980's. I thought by using a few old contacts, l may be able to rekindle this relationship, carry out our training trip and put the MRS back in touch with these top blokes. So with 4 days' worth of phone calls to USAF 56 Rescue Squadron, RAF MRS, RAF Kinloss Nimrod planners, Army barracks at Bicester, HQ Strike Command adventurous training policy and letters to the Icelandic government, our first training trip, Exercise Cold Feet was planned to complete 10 days in Iceland in November 2005.

The next battle now commenced, which was to justify why the military equipment at Bicester wasn't going to be adequate for the main goal of Antarctica. This was like facing a 1000 foot vertical ice climb, with one ice axe and crampons with no front points, as everything came down to money. The problem was, I only had authority from RAF Command to train in Iceland; I was not in a position to finance the purchasing of our own equipment and without the expertise within the military to verify my request, this vertical ice fall, remained stationary in front of me. After a long discussion with the team, we decided to follow the antiquated military way of achieving the objective, simply, carry out the task with the equipment provided and then build a case of requirement, hoping that none of my team would be injured in the process. Then Pita brought a possible second ice axe and front pointed crampons to the equation. He had made through a friend of a friend a connection with one of the UK's leading explorers, David Hempleman-Adams OBE, MBE, who had previously advised a military expedition in the past with their attempts at the North Pole. As a successful businessman and explorer, you can imagine tracking David down was extremely difficult, but once our request for an interview had been aired, our appointment was booked and we quickly drove down to Corsham to visit him.

Wanting to look as professional as possible in front of David, the team met up the previous evening, to pose a selected choice of questions to him in a sequential order that at least made sense to us. With the initial introductions behind us, we sat in David's boardroom, surrounded by pictures of his previous expeditions including his flight above Mount Everest in a wicker basket and the original maps of his unsupported expedition to the South Pole, this was the closest we had been to anyone who had actually been there and got the t-shirt! After posing the first couple of questions reference timings and route, David deliberately slapped the table with his sledge like hand and bluntly quoted that he had all the answers that we needed, but what was in it for him? As I consider myself a bounding confident person, I was taken back a gasp as to his directness, but quickly replied with a question to his question, what do you give someone who has climbed the worlds 7 highest summits, flown over Mt Everest in a balloon and solo walked to both the North and South Pole? With his beaming smile that we came accustomed to over the next 2 years, he politely replied, yeah those feats are all well and good but I've never flown in a RAF fast jet. Immediately my thoughts went back to my mountain rescue days, where having witnessed more RAF jets crashing, it was becoming increasingly harder to organise a back seat experience in any fast jet, especially for a civilian. Within these couple of milli-seconds of mulling the idea around, Pita broke the silence, by replying, yeah that's no problem; we'll just need to work on a date. Oh what had he promised, as none of us within that room had the authority to agree to such a request? David's positive response was clear and having Pita's verbal agreement to his request, he then continued to answer all of our pre-prepared questions over the next 2 hours. As the answers flowed, I could see the volume of notes equating to more work adding up; if I didn't have enough to do, with arranging all the training expeditions and the South Pole trip itself.

What was transparently clear now, I now had someone to verify that the expedition needed specialist equipment to head South, but as we were already committed to use Bicester's kit for Iceland, we would stick to plan A, use it, then prove its inefficiency. The second major win that came from the meeting with David; as he was the Chairman of the Duke of Edinburgh's Award scheme, bold as brass, I had asked him to approach Prince Phillip, requesting his thoughts on taking on the position of the expedition's Royal patron. If this was to come to fruition, the stature and leverage Prince Phillip would provide, would make some of the less reliable people, I had already come across, react more positively.

The decision from Buckingham Palace came back in less than 3 weeks, Prince Phillip had agreed. This gave me such a boost of confidence, as it proved that David had been sufficiently confident with our plan and that he believed that we could actually reach the South Pole. Secondly, I now had another hook into the RAF. As Kev Eaton was part of the RAF's recruiting team we could tell them of the connections we had with David and Prince Phillip and the Duke of Edinburgh's Award Scheme.

With this premier league level of credibility, our letters to potential sponsors now had a lot more clout. Unfortunately what we discovered over the forthcoming months was that letter writing was not the best vehicle to use when trying to source such a large amount of money. Over a period of 3 weeks, Kev Eaton sent out a tsunami of over 170 letters, which on average we received a reply from around 1 in every 15 letters sent, with companies offering discount on equipment or technical advice, but not the big bucks that I was looking for. The most effective way to source any money was by achieving a foot in the door approach into a company, then selling the expedition on what we could offer them in terms of advertisement or presentations. Finding a direct link/connection between their company, the RAF and the trip was also a crucial ingredient. As you will see later from our sponsors, the larger contributors were achieved by recognising that direct link. Something that Kev Eaton created very early on in the planning phase was a brochure containing an overview of the expedition's intentions, maps of Antarctica, potential weather, finances and training program. This brochure was an excellent vehicle not only with potential sponsors, but with anyone who took an interest in the trip so that we could relay the team's intentions to a wider audience.

While all the work was progressing with sponsorship, patronage, equipment and rations, a parallel feed of information was mandatorily required to the HQ Adventurous Training (HQAT) authority, in the end, it was these people that was going to authorise the expedition or not. Something that really helped me was knowing the characters involved and having a good level of understanding that meant we could work together, rather than me having an even bigger uphill struggle.

As no RAF expedition had ever actually reached Antarctica, they had no previous history to fall back on or use as a template to guide me. So you can see the importance of getting David Hempleman Adams on board, as his word was gospel and a perfect starting block to build from. The one thing I remember that was emphasised more than any other aspect was to ensure that the final team chosen must not only be highly trained but most of all, it must be gelled together. This from a military aspect under a disciplined organisational structure would normally never come under question, but as Antarctica clearly has no respect for rank, the team must work as one, with any major under pinning decision being left to me the expedition leader. In order to keep Command content, I would regularly provide updates on the program of weekend training exercises and the major overseas training expeditions I intended to organise in order to achieve our ultimate goal. The penciled plan consisted of the following:

November 2005	Exercise Cold Feet, Vatnajokull Glacier, Iceland
April 2006	Exercise Atlantic Ice, Langjokull Glacier, Iceland
August 2006	Exercise Norwegian Lights, Norway
Weekend training	Up to 8 exercises in Wales, Scotland and England
Daily training	Including tyre pulling and long distance running.

To organise any expedition following military procedures can take up to 6 months per expedition. The usual delays routinely fallout from waiting for authority from the Physical Education Officer (PEdO), who requires every i dotted and t crossed at least 3 times to ensure that every eventually had been considered before the whole administration process is then pushed up to the Station Commander (an equivalent Managing Director) for him or her to over sign the whole shebang. This is also where the authority for the majority of the finances required to support the trip also come from. Running sequentially with this hurry up and wait approach, is the diplomatic clearance required from the host country to allow a military exercise to take place in their country. Incredibly we had to prove and guarantee that we wouldn't be taking or using weapons to achieve our aim. Obviously each country need as much notice as possible, in some cases up to 6 months prior notification, so trying to encourage the Station Commander to sign the paperwork under his/her mountain of other work was a task in itself. One other weakened link adding to the weight of this ever increasing work load is that in my experience no two PEdO's fill in the paperwork the same way, so the burden of processing the paperwork for each expedition was going to be easier if I held it all at High Wycombe. This radical but sensible idea, took some persuasion but each of the 5 RAF stations involved came on board, as it was saving them work. Once the expedition application was signed and approved, the final step is to send your application to the Command HQAT also based at High Wycombe who gives the expedition the final seal of approval. This meant that if there were any last minute problems arise with the paperwork I could resolve them immediately as they were only across the road from my office.

My plan was simple but immense, I would work through the nausea of paperwork for the first Iceland training expedition, Exercise Cold Feet, get it approved, then before submitting it to HQAT, I would amend with the new details and submit the paperwork for Exercise Atlantic Ice to keep the momentum going. Meanwhile as each batch of expedition paperwork was returned completed, I would keep nibbling away at the major application for Antarctica herself. Reading this back in only 6 lines, looks so simple, but when you throw in, my full time job within communications, a change in PEdO and then Station Commander, attending sponsorship meetings, monitoring the progress of the team's tasks, daily training and trying to live a life with Clare my partner, resulted with life being lived at over 100 mph.

Interspersing the submission of this first application for Exercise Cold Feet, was the ball breaking effort required to order all of the equipment required through the Army supply depot at Bicester based near Oxford, knowing whole heartedly that the kit, which I must say is first class was not appropriate for our ultimate goal. The staff at Ministry of Defence (MoD) Bicester were outstanding but were obviously stuck between a rock and a hard place, as they had extremely strict protocols to adhere to, regardless to my obvious concerns. It was with their support and Phil Mainprize who had volunteered to become the team's equipment manager that the kit was provided for this trip. Phil took the bull by the horns and simultaneously started a parallel list of essential equipment for us to purchase. Knowing confidently Phil had grasped this task so well, took a mammoth amount of work off my shoulders. The team was already working superbly in their various areas.

I've only briefly mentioned training, but this was the aspect that was going to make life so much more bearable on the ice and possibly make or break our attempt. The key issue was how to simulate the physical action of pulling a sledge of around 200 lbs. The muscle groups to be educated varied from the calf, hamstring, base of spine, neck, shoulders and forearms. Not forgetting that if anyone of us was to encounter a muscular problem at any time on the ice, the expedition would be over. The historic and proven exercise to achieve this was by pulling car tyres, using a makeshift harness from an old rucksack, tying two ropes to the waist line and then tying them to the top of a tyre. My first enquiry back in June into the mechanical transport bay at RAF High Wycombe was of shear disbelief that I was firstly crazy enough to ask for a Land Rover tyre but secondly as he watched me connecting it to my rucksack, he thought I had completely lost the plot of reality. As I left the tyre bay pulling this ludicrous weight for the first time, I was so excited, full of adrenaline and relieved that my real training for our ultimate goal had actually started. Having 4 months before our first training trip to Iceland I set a program of pulling the tyre 4 times a week with 7 mile runs on the other days, with a minimum 10 mile run at the weekend. After the 5th week I added another tyre and half a concrete pavement slab balanced on top to create a pull of 220 lbs.

To me it was obvious why I was staggering around the beautiful local countryside villages of Naphill and Lacey Green, towing these tyres using 2 ski poles to maintain my balance. But to the innocent pedestrian and people who were driving past, they would gaze at me, like I had 3 heads. The funniest occasions would be seeing someone walking towards me on the same side of the road. As they got closer, they realised what I was doing and would change sides of the road, just so they didn't have to ask me that obvious question as to what the hell was I doing. The more confident people would either ask me or simply say hello and pass by like nothing was out of the ordinary. I received many verbal suggestions, for example, I should have joined the RAC or Britannia Rescue, or that if I turned the tyre on its end as it was on a car it would run a lot easier. The best comment came from an Army Major who watched me staggering through the camp gates, having just completed 3½ hours of pulling my tyre over 8 miles in 20 degrees. The sweat was pouring off me rather than dripping, he turned around after looking at my disfigured face of determination to finish off the day's training and quoted "that he felt the exact same emotions written all over my face, each time he came to work at HQ Strike Command, except that he didn't have to pull a bloody tyre to feel that way". I was left motionless, laughing so hard that I couldn't move. He kindly gave me a hand over the last 50 metres, finally shaking my soaking wet hand out of respect as he hadn't realised just how much weight was being pulled by dragging these tyres and concrete.

With under 3 weeks before departure for Exercise Cold Feet, everything apart from diplomatic clearance had been sorted; fortunately with 3 days to spare we received the fax, that our expedition had been approved. The other main issue was trying to keep my head above water with my full time job working within communications. Without the outstanding support from the COMSEC team, I would not have been in a position to organise the expedition, let alone being released to attend it. All the crypto guys were very fit and recognised that I had to increase my training schedule, which now included a 2 hour dinner break. Knowing I had the incredible support from all the guys removed an immense amount of pressure, so the more they covered for me in my absence, the more tea I made and more chocolate bar and cakes appeared at each tea break.

So, 16 months since the original conception of the idea, the South Pole candidates were ready and fully equipped to set foot on the glaciers of Iceland.

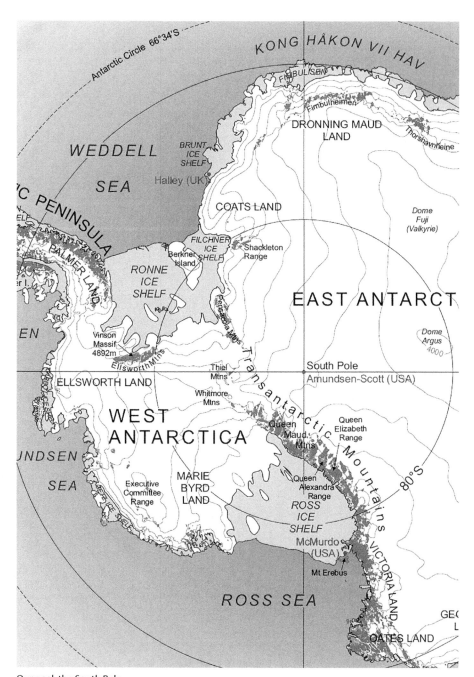

Our goal, the South Pole.

From: Brigadier Sir Miles Hunt-Davis, K.C.V.O., C.B.E.
      Private Secretary to H.R.H. The Duke of Edinburgh

BUCKINGHAM PALACE

31st January, 2006.

My dear David,

The Duke of Edinburgh has asked me to thank you for your letter dated 23rd January.

His Royal Highness has considered your request and has agreed to become Patron of the Royal Air Force team's expedition to the Geographic South Pole in September this year.

Prince Philip has, however, commented that he is not prepared to take on any further patronage commitments after this one.

As ever,

Miles

David Hempleman-Adams, Esq., O.B.E.
Executive Chairman, 50th Anniversary Programme
The Duke of Edinburgh's Award

BUCKINGHAM PALACE, LONDON. SW1A 1AA
TELEPHONE: 020 7930 4832 FACSIMILE: 020 7839 5402

Prince Philip's agreement to become the Patron of our expedition gave me a massive boost.

Chapter 2
Exercise Cold Feet

RAF Iceland Expedition, 5 November - 14 November 2005

This part of the book is a redacted version of the official post expedition report from our first overseas training visit to Iceland.

Aim
The aim of exercise Cold Feet was to form part of the training schedule for the Royal Air Force major forthcoming expedition to the Geographic South Pole in November 2006. It also contributed towards the selected team members on enhancing their leadership, fitness, self-reliance, initiative, courage and teamwork.

Objectives
To take a team of personnel already selected from 18 RAF candidates and test various equipment, communications, first aid items and build upon their skiing skills while towing a sledge and to trial a varied menu of food.

Itinerary
The expedition did not set out with a specific intention of any particular route but more to practice and build upon the team's outdoor admin skills and teamwork. As you can read from the personnel diary attached the team achieved a variety of tasks in some testing weather conditions.

Support
The support from USAF 56th Rescue Squadron cannot be emphasised enough. From the team's arrival and throughout our stay in Iceland their support was exceptional, thus allowing the expedition to achieve far more than had originally been planned.

Equipment

The expedition borrowed an immense amount of equipment from Bicester; this allowed us to trial a mass variety of items. Although it was noted that some of the equipment borrowed does need to be closely checked before its use. This does not have any reflection on the support provided by Defence Storage and Distribution Centre (DSDC) buildings C17 and C32 whom I highly commend for their advice and guidance given throughout the preparation of the expedition.

Finances

The experienced gained from our first training phase in Iceland and the financial support from each participating station was first class. The expedition raised sufficient funds to successfully achieve all of its aims.

Nominal Roll

The following personnel participated in Exercise Cold Feet:

- Sqn Ldr Kev Eaton, *RAF Cranwell*
- WO Al Sylvester, *Headquarters Strike Command, High Wycombe*
- Sgt Ian Stewart, *RAF Leuchars*
- Cpl Mike Beverage, *RAF Leuchars*
- Cpl Iain Kirk, *RAF Kinloss*
- Cpl Phil Mainprize, *RAF Halton*
- Pita, *RAF*

Top tips for future expeditions compiled by both this expedition and members of the 56th RQS:

Catering
- Boil in the bag, although has good calorific value, it too heavy and creates too much waste to carry
- A platform to cook on in the tent is required
- Dry food, either Mountain House or Arctic rations are excellent
- Nuts/raisins/chocolate chips are great while on the move
- Banana chips are not so good!!
- Unwrap as much as possible before use, saves on waste to carry.

Water
- Nalgene water bottle insulators are a must
- Put snow in Nalgene at night to melt in the warmth of your sleeping bag
- Hot water to be put in your Nalgene in the day means you can melt snow all day to top it up
- Have a sponge per tent.

Stove
- Ensure quality of fuel before departure
- A lighter per stove is good, but also important to have waterproof matches for emergency.

Sledges/Skis
- Bring extra pins for harnesses
- Consider waxing sledges before use
- Ensure all kit is enclosed in dry bags, not plastic bags
- Bring Leatherman to service bindings each evening
- Glue skins on in controlled environment. In Antarctica the skins will be screwed on.

Sleeping
- Double thickness Karrimats are to be used
- Let the sleeping bag do the work, wear minimal clothes
- Put damp items in your bag overnight in order to dry them using your body heat.

Miscellaneous
- Bring strong plastic bags to hold snow in for melting
- Bring orange Karrimor bivvy bags to put under the tents, to save the wear on ground sheet
- Pee bottles are a must
- Carry 3 snow stakes per tent
- Pay excess baggage with initial airfare, it is so much cheaper
- Bring a 10 man Zarski emergency shelter for breaks and emergencies
- Take photos through a ski goggle for amazing effects
- 'Stay-dry bags' of various sizes are essential.

The diary below gives a detailed personal account of the events that took place during Exercise Cold Feet.

Saturday 5 Nov 05

All the troops set off from their various stations, to rendezvous at Terminal 3, London Heathrow airport. On arrival Phil and I doubled up on the trolleys to convey all the equipment we had borrowed from Bicester into the foyer of T3. Moving 7 lots of equipment across 2 roads at a busy terminal certainly tested our trolley moving skills to the max. As the troops arrived we were soon to discover that Iceland Air maintain very strict guidelines with respect to excess baggage. This cost us over £300, which stretched our sense of humours, although as you will read on our return leg, there was much more fun to come. After a pretty uneventful flight, with food provided to fill a child, we were met at Keflavik airport by 2 representatives of the 56th RQS, Master Sergeant Ken Howk, who was their leader and Master Sergeant Eric Barry who both welcomed us to Iceland and immediately took us to the military base encapsulated within the Keflavik airport. The accommodation was first class, providing all the comforts of a 4 star hotel. With our stomachs rumbling for food, we were pointed in the direction of the "Chow hall", basically our equivalent to a junior ranks mess. Here we were treated to an excellent all you could eat for $3; the team were now back on top form, with full stomachs.

Back at the accommodation we held a wee meeting to discuss our plans for the next 2 days and concluded this with a beer or 3 in the local pub on base. We were once again joined by guys who hosted us throughout the evening, explaining the protocols to be followed, while sampling the local alcohol. Our arrival generated lots of interest as we were also joined by most of the 56th RQS team and their fellow helicopter crews, as you can imagine an excellent night was had by all.

Sunday 6 Nov 05

After a great overnight recovery in our luxury accommodation, Ken and the guys took us to a brunch bar, where the troops demolished a $9 all you can eat breakfast, this was the perfect remedy from the previous night's entertainment. From here Ken allowed us full use of his sections facilities to pack our sledges which he kindly loaned us. This took several hours especially concentrating on the various rations that we were going to trial over the forthcoming week on the glacier. Eric Barry then provided us an excellent DVD of a previous expedition that had crossed the Vatnajokull Glacier, followed by pictures that his troops had taken only 2 weeks before during their training mission. This really wet our appetite creating even more excitement for our training ahead. After a visit to the US Navy BX (a BX is the equivalent of our NAAFI, except better and a lot cheaper), Ken and his wife Heather kindly invited our team over to their home for a meal. This once again highlights the outstanding level of sincerity of the support we received throughout our stay. With a 0315 hours start beckoning us, we passed on our gratitude and said our farewells to Ken's family and headed back to accommodation for our last night of comfort in a proper bed for the next few days.

Monday 7 Nov 05

Due to work commitments Pita was unable to join us on the glacier part of the expedition. Before his flight back, he touched base with the rescue helicopter squadron and had smoothed the path to possibly use the Black Hawk helicopters as a means as transport for any future expeditions to Iceland. Taking a last shower seemed to take an age, as from now on our cleanliness would be down to baby wipes and glacial water. Ken and Josh picked the troops up in 2 huge USAF trucks at 0330 hours as planned, and our journey to the drop off point began. With just a little over 5 hours travelled we arrived at the drop off point just as dawn was breaking. Unfortunately due to the track conditions, we were too far away from the glacier so we traveled a further hour passing Glacier Bay, which is an incredible phenomenon, with icebergs being hosted in a tight bay of glacial water.

Shortly after we arrived at our second drop off location we were met with more snow and icy tracks. As Ken and Josh could go any further, we said our fond farewells and set about carrying our sledges for the next 2 hours until we finally arrived at the glaciers snout. It was now we all recognised the benefits of Heather's spinach lasagna we had eaten the previous evening as our forearms, felt like Popeye's. Using the rope to lower the sledges onto the glacier, at long last we got our chance to put into practice all the training we had achieved so far with dragging our tyres around back in the UK. As we carefully navigated through the crevasse field we travelled for around 3 hours where we found a suitable location for our base camp. With the tents and a wee wind shelter wall erected we settled down for a brew and debriefed the day's events. Tonight I tried out some the dried food given to us from Ken, a beef teriyaki and rice mixture, which was superb. Most importantly was the weight of the package and the nutritional value of the food, this was awesome, in comparison to the boil in the bag food; we had been forced to bring with us. As a pudding, Mike and Ian shared a huge container of peanuts; the team demolished them in minutes. While cooking it was noted that one of the MSR cookers was producing lots of carbon deposits and clogging up the jets. Even after cleaning and servicing it, it still wasn't firing on all cylinders.

Weather: Overcast with occasional rain, reasonable visibility with light winds. Temperature approx -5 degrees.

Tuesday 8 Nov 05

Using the flasks we had made up the previous night, a warm drink was enjoyed by all before fully opening our sleeping bags, to feel the full bitterness of the cold temperature. The inside of the Quazer tent was frozen which added to the atmosphere of the tent. Although one of our cookers was still playing up, Mike and I used our other cooker to boil the water for our boil in the bags, which produced a tasty bacon and beans breakfast. Next task was to melt enough ice to provide boiling water for our flasks, ahead of our day.

Leaving our tents behind, we set off to concentrate on our skiing skills whilst towing a fully loaded sledge. The first hour was spent walking in crampons while we circumnavigated around a rather spicy crevasse field. The snow that had covered the surface yesterday had blown away and with the freezing temperatures had covered the glacier in a glaze of ice. Once clear we donned our skis and pick up a reasonable pace. The benefits of our training really made a huge difference to our legs and back muscles. We were blessed with great weather which provided us all with incredible views of the beautiful glaciers and mountains that surrounded us. It also gave us a possible plan for tomorrow's route, which would take in a wee hut and then onto a superb mountain range in the distance. After a short lunch break we reciprocated our route back to our tents. With 90 mins of light left, we utilised the time to sample 30 foot of front pointing ice climbing within a crevasse close by. Looking at the faces of the team, they had all enjoyed a great first day on the ice.

After discussing the situation regarding the unserviceable cooker, it was decided to just use the one cooker and save wasting any fuel. While cooking, 2 troops stripped the cooker down to its bare bones, but unfortunately to no avail. It had been a huge learning curve, realising the importance of its loss.

After sampling both dried food and boil in the bags, we discussed the events of the day, good and bad points, followed by a game of travel monopoly. Unfortunately during the evening the erratic violent smells being produced by the effects of composite rations, came too much for everyone and I was banished to a crevassed to resolve the problem. It was only on my return that Kirky advised me that he estimated the outside temperature was around 25 degrees below, which was rather refreshing. Thankfully, I was sheltered from the wind while resolving the smell problem. After concluding monopoly, everyone sank into the sleeping bags for a great night's sleep.

Weather: Excellent throughout the day, but with clear skies, the temperatures dropped dramatically at night.

Wednesday 9 Nov 05

Awaking this time at 0700 hours, we worked in the dark as sunrise wasn't until 0840 hours. With only 1 cooker, it took 90 mins to complete everyone's breakfast. It was also during conversations with the team that I noted that none of us were drinking enough water, as individuals were showing signs of dehydration. The frustrating time taken to heat all the boil in the bags and the immense weight was enough for me to prove to Command Catering that, we needed dry rations. We packed up base camp and moved everything, leaving behind only pee, poo and footprints.

Taking the same route in crampons, we quickly moved through the crevasse field this time heading for the wee hut seen the previous day. As we donned skis again, the weather took a turn for the worse, as the visibility dropped to around 10 metres with the cloud thickening and the snow beginning to fall. Within 3 hours, conditions deteriorated further, resulting with the decision to descend from the side of the mountain and erect a base camp with a sense of urgency. On arrival the team performed extremely well under their first real test against the elements by getting both tents up and having the water boiling for a well earned brew in less than an hour. 8 inches of snow fell in 6 hours, resulting with a relay of volunteers digging the top layer of snow off the tents as they bowed under the weight of the cold dry snow. The other reason, apart from character building troops who had never experienced this environment, is if you don't clear the snow, you'll eventually suffocate!! Also for the first time today, we had utilised our Global Positioning System (Garmin Etrex) to great effect. I was happy with our navigation today, but as Antarctica is virtually featureless the Garmin was going to be our life line down South. Following a game of cards and a hot debrief on the day's events, the troops sampled more culinary delights before having an early night. Not forgetting the relay of volunteers to dig the tent out around every 2 hours throughout the night.

Weather: Started off clear but rapidly deteriorated in the afternoon. Heavy snow and strong winds, also added to the interesting conditions.

Thursday 10 Nov 05

After waking shortly before 0600 hours, the numb airy silence outside meant we were either completely cocooned in snow or the wind had dropped; it was like waking up in a snow hole. Well, fortunately the wind had dropped but another 6 inches of snow had fallen in the night. So our first job was to dig out the sledges while lucky Mike got on with melting some snow for breakfast. It was encouraging to see the teams' admin skills were speeding up as we struck the tents and prepared to set off just as first light appeared. We set off in extremely deep snow in an Easterly direction in approximately 5 metres of visibility. The Garmin came into its element again, as we had marked several way points the previous day to help us to reciprocate our route. Unfortunately during my lead, I led my sledge into a rather sporty ridge area of a crevasse that ensured I used a couple of extra heart beats to recover myself back to the amusement of my waiting team. From here we circumnavigated around the main crevasse field, working our sledges through very deep snow, which tested both our patience and strength. As we descended the sun burnt away the thick mist to provide us the best views of the expedition so far. We could literally see for miles, including the illusive hut we had been navigating towards yesterday. With clear visibility we increased our speed, experiencing our first taste of downhill skiing with a sledge in tow; wow, there is very little room for error.

As we pulled up at our starting up, the 12 inches of snow allowed us easy access back to the rocks we had previously had to carry the sledges over. This time we could simply pull our sledge back down the track. Realising the 56th RQS troops would not get their wagons up the track; we started a 7 kms pull until reaching a suitable base camp area, with an outstanding view of an Icelandic sunset. With the tents up and the cooker on, we played Star Wars trump cards until it was time to sample our last dried food offering, a chicken stew, a sweet and sour meal and a curry, all of which got the thumbs up and will be used on our menu for the South Pole next year. We concluded the evening with a debrief of our expedition which we all agreed had been a resounding success, with lots of tops tips being picked up along the way.

Weather: Firstly whiteout, but cleared into an exceptional great day with temperatures around -10 degrees. With clear skies in the evening, the temperature naturally dropped to around -18 with an increasing wind.

Friday 11 Nov 05
Knowing the 56th RQS were on route, we packed up base camp and using the patches of ice on the track, we pulled the sledges a further 2 kms closer to the road. From this point Kev and I left the sledges behind and walked the remaining 6 kms to the road head, where we met up with Josh, Skye and Jake in their huge pickup trucks. As this was Armistice Day, although the team were separated at 1100 hours, all of the guys at their various locations had paid their respects to our fallen heroes, by standing in silence for 2 minutes.

The guys made light work of the icy track and ploughed through until we collected the sledges and remainder of the team. With us all loaded, within 20 mins we stopped at Glacier Bay, which we had clocked as a place of incredible beauty on the way. The guys had not only stopped for us to take photos but for Jake who had served with them for around 8 months in Iceland, was bet $60 to lay in his birthday suit in the icy waters for 2 minutes. If Jake succeeded he could also adopt a new callsign Polar Bear. The first minute we watched Jake laughing and joking with his mates but as the second minute passed by, Jake started to struggle moving his arms and legs, he started to gasp for air, while his mates looked on laughing thinking about their $60. As 120 seconds concluded, Jake really struggled to crawl out of his Icelandic ice bath, but we were not allowed to help him. Struggling to breathe, he boasted about his new callsign and then remembered the $60 he had just earned himself. Not bad for 2 minutes work!!

On the way home we stopped off at a garage and I treated all the guys to a burger, chips and drink. We were definitely in Iceland as the bill for the 10 of us was over £110, hey who thinks Burger King isn't value for money?

The closer we got to Keflavik the more the weather deteriorated again, with 40 mph winds whipping across the already frozen roads. At 2100 hours we pulled into camp, to be met by Ken at the section. Although not wanting to abuse the hospitality already shown to us, Ken very kindly offered the use of his section again so we may unload our soaking and now defrosted equipment. This was an absolute godsend. From here with our kit sorted, we all headed back to the luxury of our rooms and a glorious shower. We concluded the night by sneaking in a couple of beers down the local bar, shortly followed by heading to bed for a well earned rest.

Sunday 12 November 05
Starting at 0900 hours the troops headed back to the brunch bar that sold the multi storey car park breakfasts for $9. After demolishing at last 2 plates worth each, we all headed off to the BX for a wee final shopping spree, buying all those things that you don't really want but as there cheaper than in the UK, it would be rude not to.

Shortly after 1300 hours Skye and Jake picked the team up and drove us to the Blue Lagoon, which is an incredible Sulphur spring complex. The set of pools, waterfalls and saunas is outstanding, with the added bonus of trying some organic cream substance over your skin. It basically looked and felt like rubbing porridge into your skin, believe me it never improved the looks of any of the troops. After 2 hours of sheer bliss, we headed back to 56th RQS section to pack away all our kit and prepare for the next day's flight. While packing up our kit, Kirky highlighted the painful effects of badly fitting ski boots, the result of which meant a trip to the US Navy medical centre as the broken blisters and bruising looked extremely painful. After an antibiotic injection and the wounds being covered in fresh dressing, he returned with some great photos providing evidence of just how bad they were. Back in our rooms, the troops chilled out watching England beat Argentina 3 v 2 to everyone's pleasure except for our Scottish contingency, who sorrowfully smiled as also their rugby team were beaten and their football team only managed a draw. Once everyone had rested we met up with our hosts in the pizza bar on camp, where we treated the troops to pizza and beer all night. Additionally we presented Ken and the troops a few gifts to highlight our appreciation of what outstanding support the guys have provided us throughout our stay.

Sunday 14 Nov 05

After a restless night, the troops met up in the foyer at 0630 hours to be picked up by Jake and Skye who took us to the airport. As we said our goodbyes in the pouring rain, words could not express our gratitude to the troops from 56th RQS; their enthusiastic support throughout the whole of our stay had been beyond our wildest dreams. These guys have an incredible zest for life, they show outstanding professionalism with everything that they do and provide a first class representation of the US Air Force. I can honestly say that the support provided by 56th RQS was the key to the success of our expedition to Iceland. My final word of thanks goes to MSgt Ken Howk who leads the team, whom without his personal exceptional support this expedition would not have happened.

Having carefully packed our bags to minimize the excess to be paid, we were annoyed to find that although we were probably slightly over our allocated weight, we were to be charged a ski handling fee of £30 per set, which completely contradicted the protocols used at London Heathrow airport. This issue was taken up with Icelandic Airway when I returned but they refused to refund any of our money. Once back at Heathrow after an uneventful flight, everyone packaged up their equipment into separate piles to ease the burden for Phil, before he returned the equipment back to Bicester.

The expedition had set out to assess equipment, build the team spirit, improve everyone's admin knowledge and practice pulling our sledges while wearing skis. We achieved this and much more and have prepared ourselves for the next training expedition, during which we can tighten up our procedures further before setting out on our final destination of the Geographic South Pole.

Chapter 3
Phase 2: November 2005 - April 2006

Exercise Cold Feet opened my eyes to the incredible challenge the team and I still had ahead of us. As the report concludes, it achieved all its objectives and more but also a few weaknesses had become apparent. At the front of my concerns was the level of fitness. It was clear that some of the guys had a natural level of fitness but others were going to have to work bloody hard to reach the level that I was demanding. It was not just speed, but more importantly, it was the weight that we were training with had to be increased to simulate what we would be pulling for 7 weeks down south.

On the day I returned to work, I ventured down to the mechanical transport section again, only to find that they could only give me another Land Rover tyre which was far too heavy. It was while driving to Clare's house that night I remember that during my last 12 mile run the previous weekend, I had past some tyres that had been dumped on the side of the road. So I diverted off my normal route to Clare's to find my new pulling companion. It didn't take long to find it as the winter had killed off lots of greenery in the ditches making it easy to see. I picked up my Vauxhall Astra sized tyre, stuck it in the boot and carried on Clare's to tell her about my new friend.

Clare and I had now known each other around 4 months and fortunately for me, I was already working on the expedition when I first met her at Dean's house in Swindon in August. The drive between High Wycombe and Swindon, although taking me around 90 mins each way, gave me time to muddle through, the achievements of the day and then to work on what was next on the agenda. As a Police Officer, Clare's shifts appeared to be laid out by Stevie Wonder with a catapult, as I couldn't keep track of when she was working or not. Thank goodness for mobile phones, this saved me the journey through on more than one occasion. Clare had the patience of a saint, as if I wasn't working on South Pole admin, I would be talking to her about it and asking what she would do. Which looking back was crazy as Clare doesn't have a mountaineering bone in her body. At least it maintained her interest in the expedition and me for being so barmy for attempting such a feat.

2 Dec 05

Trying to keep the team together and informed of the latest goings was extremely difficult, as I had 7 troops from 6 different RAF stations. Some were on the internet, some weren't, which resulted in me not getting information to them quick enough, causing me great frustration. Fortunately at the beginning of December we had one of our weekend training meetings in Feshiebridge, a fantastic bothy in the heart of the Highlands and at the foot of the Cairngorms. Ian and Mike were based at RAF Leuchars, so I had tasked them to organise this training weekend. The weekend was split up into 3 parts. Starting on Friday evening, we discussed the latest successes and what had been achieved over the past 2 months; this was achieved while simultaneously introducing the troops to a 12 year malt whisky called Highland Park. It was transparent as the troops fed back their updates as to who had been researching and working on some of the more mundane tasks. From my perspective it wasn't just the physical performance on the mountain that counted, but the enthusiasm and determination shown with their delegated tasks. I knew that I was flat out, working late virtually every evening trying to get us to Antarctica, if the troops were not reciprocating, why should they remain as part of my team. There were tasks that had not progressed quickly enough; hence I gave those individuals a little kick up the backside.

The 3 major aspects now was to source the expeditions own equipment, start work on calorific values of dried food and of course money, we still needed over £160K.

Phil had the list of equipment which we knew could borrow from Bicester but also he had the ever increasing list of light weight kit required, that the expedition would have to pay for. It was during one of his many nights researching kit on the internet, that he made contact with of the 5 ladies who had reached the South Pole back in 2000. Zoe Hudson works out of London and offered up various dates that she would be available to meet up with the team. Phil excitedly phoned me telling me the great news. This was outstanding news, as having both David's advice and now Zoe's, another recognised explorer on board, this would certainly put the minds of HQAT at rest.

February 2006

At the beginning of the month, Kirky had been selected to serve another 5 months out on Operation Telic, serving in Basra, Iraq again. This time, he was regularly spotted pulling tyres around the inner perimeter of the secure base. You can imagine the looks he got, especially when the temperatures were even hotter than his first time, at 45 degrees.

To get the troops off again for a single event could start to annoy the teams working colleagues, so to further raise the importance of the trip to London, I arranged a meeting with the Foreign Commonwealth Office (FCO) who govern the diplomatic clearance for British people who want to visit and stay on Antarctica.

With the team coming from various locations, we arranged to meet at Paddington railway station and then made our way via a very busy tube to Embankment station, where we walked past Downing Street to reach the FCO. This magnificent building demanding respect from its neighbourhood, added to my butterflies in my stomach, as once again, we were promoting our expedition to another senior organisation. My major fear was we were requesting authority for an expedition which was still £160K short and still missing the final approval from HQAT. Within minutes of meeting David Stock the FCO coordinator for Antarctica and the South Atlantic, my anxiety was eased as he welcomed the team so warmly. David explained that Antarctica was the last continent on earth that was not owned or controlled by any one country, additionally as we were a military organisation there was no requirement for us to follow the mandatory application to step foot on Antarctica. As Expedition Leader I felt that we should not abuse this position and requested that our team follow the mandatory procedures, not only to prevent any possible diplomatic situation arising while in Chile but also, I felt this was a very important aspect that the expedition should have if looked upon by any external authority or party. The team spent around an hour bleeding David dry of any information he could give from previous expeditions that he had reviewed in the past. The most interesting point raised was about the removal of human waste and that any domestic waste could not be burnt while on the ice. I had expected the domestic waste but having read into various previous expeditions, they had never been asked to carry their own poo. I was going to have to research this one a little further, as the consequences of hygiene was bouncing around my small brain. We left the FCO with the Antarctica application forms and started off across London to meet Zoe at the RAF Officer's Club, which Kev Eaton had gained permission for the team non – officers to have a meal.

As we waited in reception all smartly dressed in suits, I could not help think with the comparison as to what we will look like after having spent 7 weeks on the ice. Within a short time Zoe arrived with radiating smiles and enthusiasm with every breath. As we sat around our table, all of us were eager to ask lots of questions but as Phil's guest, he took the lead primarily asking about equipment, which I noticed he cleverly compared Zoe's answers to David Hempleman-Adams, which not only verified David's advice but further enhanced the detail. Zoe presented herself in a very relaxed manor but as we maintained this barrage of questions, we noticed as we had finished our starters, poor Zoe had hardly had time to touch hers, as she was so busy answering our questions. As the main course arrived, we calmed our enthusiasm to allow everyone a pleasant meal while still absorbing lots of information on a huge array of topics. One question that stuck in my mind and I posed, was how did Zoe feel as she finally reached the South Pole. With a respectful moment of silence, she raised her napkin to her mouth, cleared her lips and quietly replied, I won't answer that Al, as I would like to know how you feel when you reach there and then we can compare our answers. That answer made me feel a million dollars, as the 2 hours that we had spent with Zoe had given her enough confidence to believe that our team did have the potential to go the whole way. Finishing off the meal with a coffee, we said our farewells, having experienced a lovely evening with a charming lady who despite her small stature had the strength of character and determination which was second to none.

A huge aspect of discussion that came from our evening with Zoe was the expedition's food. Mike Beveridge had been delegated to research food so with all the new information from Zoe, Mike now had to set out to approach various firms who specialised in dry food. Another task was to assess the calorific values of various chocolate bars to see which would give us the greater value with the minimum weight. Zoe had quoted that she had taken 15 kms of chocolate but that had not been enough! At the time I thought this was a little excessive, but when you think about it a little deeper when you distribute that over 7 weeks, it's not a lot really.

Mike's research came across a company called First Choice Expedition Foods. They provided a similar variety of dried packed food that we'd borrowed from Ken and the guys in Iceland, so we could enjoy curry's, sweet and sours, hot pots, chilli con carne, the list was very promising. Most importantly they were distributers of the calorie filled Pemmikan. Pemmikan is a highly condensed form of food made from dried and ground meat mixed with a similar weight of fat, even a small amount provides a lot of energy, it is almost entirely protein and fat with very little carbohydrate. What this description doesn't highlight is, it tastes gopping. Regardless of how you describe it, boil it, fry it, chew on it, Pemmikan is bloody awful but it does contain gallons of calories, which will be essential.

March 2006

One person who was in almost daily contact with me was Phil. He had been working tirelessly to compose a list of equipment that we would need to buy that was not available from our service source at Bicester. As the clocked ticked closer to our next training adventure back to Iceland and after weeks of researching previous Antarctic expeditions, Phil emailed me his wish list. Within seconds of him pressing send, my phone rang. Phil in his infectious manner, asked me to open my email. Laughing as we almost always did, my eyes were drawn to the bottom figure of almost £4,500! At this time the expedition only had just under £5K available for kit in the bank and Phil wanted it all. As Phil talked highlighting how the team's safety would be at risk if we didn't purchase the right equipment, all I could think about was spending the money on an expedition that hadn't even been approved yet. Oh and there was also the fact that I had to raise approximately another £140K before we leave. Without letting on, I said to Phil, let's do it, where is the kit on sale. Phil then immediately burst out laughing, "that's another thing Al, I've got to go to

Oslo in Norway to pick it up". I knew now that I was already on thin ice and what I was taking was a calculated risk, but with this kit, I could promote our expedition further and highlight the costs that I've already incurred. Over the next few weeks, it paid off. The only slight hick up came was when Phil tried to exchange £4,500 into Norwegian Krona at a Thomas Cook travel agency. While at work one morning, Phil called me explaining that he was under suspicion of money laundering as he was trying to exchange such a large amount of cash. To resolve the situation, I spoke to the staff and then sent a letter via fax with our Patrons on it explaining what Phil was trying to achieve. Thankfully, they accepted my letter and let Phil proceed without any further investigation.

Phil and Pita flew across to Oslo, picked up the kit and made a saving of over £700 in comparison to purchasing the kit over here in the UK. The pain staking business case which I hand delivered to the Army's HQ at Wilton Barracks, didn't change their opinion on the quality of their kit, however as we had saved them the costs of buying new kit, they would now consider supporting my case for purchasing the sledges.

This was the only item of equipment I took responsibility for. Sledges or pulks as they are sometimes called within the explorers' vocabulary were going to be our sole mate on the ice. I had sourced 3 companies all of whom had specific features making their product the best for Antarctica. After some lengthy discussions, I concluded that Fjellpulken had the best reputation and were the most robust sledge to endure the 7 weeks of battering and bruising ahead of us. The deciding factor that sealed my decision was if I had chosen the lighter more flimsy model and it broke during our attempt, the expedition would be over, as we would not be in a position to repair it, regardless of what spares we were being advised to carry in the event of a crack or tear. Additionally the countless previous expeditions that had chosen this make, also gave me the confidence that I had made the right choice. As the Army HQ were considering sharing the costs and knowing Phil had spent virtually all of the expedition's money, I politely stalled them, saying the cost of taking them over to Iceland in a few weeks would be too excessive. Thankfully, they believed me.

Realising that money was a severe issue I spoke to Kev Eaton to see what our options were as we desperately needed companies to buy in. Kev had received some support to date, but we realised that we needed to target companies who were working directly with or for the RAF. Kev and I compiled a list, sent it out to the team and asked them to add to it. The team came up trumps with several great ideas and bids were submitted to the RAF Sports Lottery, Nuffield Trust and RAF Regiment. Over a period of the next 6 months this opened several doors, but it was a very anxious wait to watch the money coming in slower than a tortoise on reheat.

The other avenue was for me to ask Sir Brian to sign off a letter requesting RAF stations with any annual underspends to consider giving it to our expedition. I knew this was a very cheeky approach, as a Station Commander receiving a letter from the Commander In Chief was almost obliged to help. With only pennies in the bank and with the teams' financial worries building; I didn't care and got on with the task of posting the letters off to the 66 establishments under Sir Brian's command. Where I recognised a Station Commander, I also added my own note offering a free presentation to generate adventurous training on their unit. In addition, I used the same envelope to send out letters and poster to all the RAF gymnasiums to raise the expedition's awareness and again to try and source more money. I must add here, the support I was personally receiving from RAF High Wycombe was outstanding. As each training expedition had to follow a strict administration chain of command to authorise each aspect i.e. food, travel, money etc, I was very fortunate to have a Station Commander, Group Captain Carol Smith MBE in overall charge. As Carol trusted the experience of the main stake holders i.e. the guys and girls in the catering section, the financiers and the team in the physical education centre it made my life so much easier. Once the expedition was authorised, I could then send it out to the troops, so they could receive the same support. This is where certain individuals who were clearly very important in their own breakfast time became a huge challenge. Trying to co-ordinate 5 RAF stations, who were supposed to be following the same procedures, was ridiculous as individually they believed that their system was the best. I wish I could calculate how many heart beats I lost appeasing so many self righteous people, all of whom eventually bowed to accept that even from their ivory tower of power they had to follow the RAF's laid down procedures. From my perspective, I was looking at the overall picture, from their perspective they were trying to penny pinch money that actually wasn't theirs!

My life

The time between the first and second Iceland trips was also incredibly busy for me, as beyond the melee of the expedition my personal life was now being pulled in every direction. As I now had a copy of Clare's shifts, we worked out the days and nights that we could see each other. This worked a treat, as Clare with all her evening/night shifts meant that I could crack on with expedition admin without feeling too guilty. But when we did see each other, although I would update her on the barrage of work I'd completed, I tried not to mention it, although my mind was still at 100 mph trying to work specific issues out. Clare was awesome as on her days off, she would drive over to stay at High Wycombe, where we made plans for our next holiday and discuss the possibilities of buying a house together. By January we'd worked out that geographically Faringdon in Oxfordshire was our favourite location and by February we had moved into our 2 bedroom terraced house in this small quiet market town; (Dean's blind date really did go well).

Regardless of what plans Clare and I had, I was still religiously maintaining my 1150 mile monthly drive to Inverness to see Kieran. I would try and speak to him every 2 days which was sometimes difficult as occasionally he was not allowed or unable to answer the phone. These weekends were so precious as although I had very little bearing in his life apart from phone calls, our weekends were so important. As my plan was to return back to Kinloss, I still owned the bungalow in Nairn (about 15 miles from Inverness), so we could always stay in the same location and give him the stability that I knew he so desperately needed. We shared great weekends together, constantly playing, catching up on wild stories but most of all maintaining our loving father and son relationship. After starting my drive in the early hours of Friday morning, picking Kieran up from school, we would be none stop, until I dropped him off at 1630 hours on Sunday before my 9 ½ hour drive back to Faringdon. Those last 4 ½ hours after passing over the Scottish border were so tiring, but Clare would religiously phone me every hour, perking me up, encouraging me to stop and ensuring that I drove home safely.

The roller coaster of emotions just continued to join the ride, as 2 weeks before our second trip to Iceland, Clare broke the new to me that she was pregnant. Clare had seen my stress levels over the previous couple of weeks starting to climb into the stratosphere, as a few agencies were becoming "more than their jobs worth" standing in the way of the expedition. So while we were away on a camping weekend in Westward Ho, Devon Clare calmly broke the news, wondering what my reaction would be. I was ecstatic, over the moon and was so happy. Then my brain felt like it was trying to decipher Japanese writing as I calmly and discreetly tried to calculate dates, months due in comparison to the start of the expedition. Clare smiled and was miles ahead as she watched my internal thoughts bounce between my ears. Together we worked out that Clare would be due in the middle of October, only 2 weeks before departure. That was it; for me the expedition was over!! On no account was I selfishly clearing off on what could be a life threatening voyage leaving behind Clare and our baby. Clare, on the other hand had other ideas. Clare's opinion was that she would be on maternity leave for the 3 months, while I would be away and apart sharing the time together as a family, I wouldn't miss out. Even writing this now, words cannot express the mental strain of guilt that was spinning around my mind, I felt physically sick. As we walked along the stunning beach hand in hand, we dropped the subject, but in my mind, the decision had been made, I'm not going. On returning to work, my mind was like the roads around Birmingham's spaghetti junction as for the first time in 18 months; my enthusiasm and drive simply stopped. Although I was withdrawing, I needed to choose another leader, so I made the decision not to tell anyone until the team returned from our second trip to Iceland. I also realised that even though I wasn't going to go to Antarctica I would still need to keep the momentum going to get the team there. Talk about being between a rock and a very hard place.

The final aspect of my personal life was training. By now, I was pulling my tyres quite comfortably between 5 – 7 hours but I was simultaneously acclimatising my body to drink less water. As something that David had mentioned and what I had noted in Iceland was dehydration. While pulling our sledges in Antarctica, we would have a limited supply of water, so what I had started to do was reduce the amount of water I drank as I pulled my tyres. A daily training session would involve pulling the tyres for around 4 hours, drinking only 1 ½ litres of water, which was down from 3 litres when I first started. It took several months to achieve this but the benefits were to come to fruition on the ice.

5 – 6 April 06

One of the tasks that had been on the back burner but needed approval was the promise we had made during our first meeting with David Hempleman-Adams, for him to experience a back seat flight in the back of a fast jet. So during one of my updates with Sir Brian, I dropped into the conversation as to how this could be authorised. With a wry smile, Sir Brian asked me to contact the Station Commander at RAF Valley on his behalf and ask him to assist us. This was a first, a Warrant Officer acting on behalf of the Commander in Chief of the RAF. Well, the expedition had come this far so I made the call.

The Station Commander was only too happy to help and guided me to one of my mountain rescue friends Flight Lieutenant Graham Duff (Duffy), who was now an instructor on the Hawk squadron at Valley. I knew Duffy as a young RAF Leuchars troop while I was the team leader at Kinloss. Now as a Hawk instructor he was the perfect man to help us. After a great catch up over the phone, Duffy happily took on the job of arranging the necessary paperwork for not only the Hawk back seat experience, but the mountain of paperwork required to host a civilian on a military establishment. Recognising David's visit had a huge publicity potential, I arranged for as many of my team to meet us at Valley. Duffy requested that David arrived the day before his flight so that he may be fitted with a flying suit, helmet and appropriate clothing. This was followed by a half an hour familiarization brief on the inside of a Hawk. As a note of appreciation to RAF Valley, David volunteered to provide a presentation on his expeditions around the world, including climbing the 7 summits and reaching both poles unsupported. The operations briefing room was packed as so many people recognised the magnitude of what David had achieved as one of the UK's leading explorers. As the RAF saying goes "no bottle to throttle" for 24 hours before a flight, everyone enjoyed a great but soberish evening in the Officer's Mess.

After a full English breakfast, David was taken to the medical centre to receive his preflight medical which he passed with flying colours. From here it was off to 208 Squadron where Duffy and my team were awaiting David's arrival for our photo opportunity. Brandishing our new "Southern Reach 2006" tee shirts, we all posed with David and Duffy in front of the Hawk before leaving Duffy to fulfil one of David's ambitions to fly in a fast jet. On landing, the smile on David's face said it all, Duffy had taken him half way around North Wales and pulled some incredible force gravity during some very tight turns and had even allowed David to fly the aircraft above the clouds. Thinking back to David's initial barefaced request, we had now fulfilled it and I felt a little more at ease using his name as our technical advisor.

Even though my position had changed from the team, the final 2 weeks before departing for Iceland the second time was full on. Problems with last minute clearance problems again and collecting unserviceable equipment from Bicester was just 2 examples. Fortunately with lots of help from Phil again, we prepared everything just in time for departure on the Saturday.

Chapter 4
Exercise Atlantic Ice
RAF Iceland Expedition, 25 April - 5 May 2006

This part of the book is a redacted version of the official post expedition report from our first overseas training visit to Iceland.

The aim, objectives, support and finances were the same as the planning for our first Icelandic training expedition; the main difference was the equipment, as now we had started to purchase some of our own equipment, which we obviously tested over the forthcoming weeks.

Nominal Roll
The following personnel participated in Exercise Atlantic Ice:

* WO Al Sylvester, *Headquarters Strike Command, High Wycombe*
* Sgt Ian Stewart, *RAF Leuchars*
* Cpl Mike Beverage, *RAF Leuchars*
* Pita, *RAF*

The diary below gives a detailed personal account of the events that took place during Exercise Atlantic Ice.

Saturday 22 Apr 06
With all the troops arriving at Heathrow airport, Terminal 2, from their various units, they immediately set upon packing the equipment loaned from DSDC Bicester. As we hesitantly approached the Icelandic Air check in desk, our fears of huge excess baggage fees were soon dissolved, as the hostess acknowledge the uniformity of the team wearing their 'Southern Reach 2006' tee shirts, very kindly wavered a large percentage of our fees. Just why they couldn't have

done that on our first expedition, Lord only knows? An uneventful flight with notably small portions of food again, soon brought us into land at Keflavik, where we were once again met by the leader of the USAF 56th RQS Pararescue Team, MSgt Ken Howk. With his huge wagon loaded with all our equipment, Ken took us to his section and then to our 5 star accommodation, where we sorted our admin out before descending on the chow hall for some great food.

Returning back to our billet, we discussed our plan for the next 2 days, watched Liverpool beat Chelsea in the Semi Final of the FA Cup and they headed to the local Station bar to meet up with the remaining members of the 56 RQS team. A chilled night was enjoyed with the guys, catching up on the latest news including the imminent closure and move to USAF Lakenheath, UK. Ken's team had been cut by half to only 6 personnel but once again as you will read, the support from his team was the crucial key to the expedition's success.

Sunday 23 Apr 06

I awoke early as my mind was bursting with so many thoughts of Clare, kit, food and money needed, so I sorted out the money for our accommodation, excess baggage, food etc. Meeting up with Ken, we set upon the stations other food hall, where we demolished a $9 all you can eat breakfast, which set us all up for a day of packing and planning.

Using 56th RQS section, we discussed at length the various layering systems to be used while out on the glacier. We have no room for error, so 3 types of head wear, 3 types of gloves, a vapour barrier system with our boots and a 5 layer next to skin system to keep us warm. With all team members working the same system it reaped many benefits, while keeping the overall weight of our pulks down. Having met up with our technical advisor David Hempleman-Adams recently at RAF Valley while receiving his Hawk flight, we followed his advice about prepping the ASNES skis and Rotafella bindings and boots. The old expression of prior preparation prevents a poor performance; certainly counted as our newly purchased equipment was first class.

With a huge grin, Ken passed a copy of the next 7 days weather to me, basically, it read, snow, gales, snow, stronger gales oh and more snow; perfect, just what we needed to put our new equipment and navigational knowledge to the test. With the 2 maps of the Langjokull glacier, the team produced a route to circumnavigate the glacier, keeping clear of the obvious crevasse areas. Our intention is to travel 7 miles for 3 days, then up the mileage to 8 miles for 3 days and then 9 to 10 miles for the remainder of our time up on the ice.

After a last minute shopping spree in the USAF BX, we came back to the billet for a wee break, giving time for the troops to write postcards to all the sections whom had helped us with not only this expedition but with our ultimate quest. At 1700 hours, Ken picked the team up and took us to one of the team members home (Coreen) who served up chilli dogs and chips, a meal to savour as from tomorrow, its dried food all the way. Virtually all of the 56th RQS team and families joined us, while we watched a movie on the standard 56 inch colour TV screen. This once again highlights the genuine wonderful hospitality from our colleagues in the USAF.

Weather: Windy, overcast with occasional snow/rain showers.

Monday 24 Apr 06
The team met up for breakfast at 0700 hours, before getting picked up by Chan and Jake, who diverted via the section to collect our fully laden pulks and then onto Keflavik to pick up some cooking fuel for our MSR stoves.

Our drive to the glacier took us via some amazing Geysers, which claims to be the second highest exploding sulphur water burst in the world. It is an incredible phenomenon, which erupts approximately every 4 to 5 mins. With lots of touristy photos taken we headed off up the road a further 10 kms, where we were greeted with a road closed sign, due to heavy snow. Using the opportunity we utilized the nearby café to discuss a plan. The shock of the water bursting 70 feet from the ground 15 mins earlier was put far into the distance with the heart stopping price of £6.50 for a bowl of soup, so we enjoyed a marginally cheaper cup of tea instead. Jake spoke to a few contacts, who advised us that the road was passable with care, so it was all systems go. Chan who had limited driving experience on icy roads did exceptionally well and carefully placed us only 7 miles short of our original drop off location. With our farewells said, Chan and Jake headed back to Keflavik, as we headed on foot to our glacier with crystal clear skies and incredible views. After only 30 minutes the depth of the snow allowed us to don our new skis and travel much quicker. Following the obvious tracks, we soon covered the 7 miles to the edge of the glacier and decided to erect camp and set up for the evening by the side of a huge alpine wooden hut. This was owned by Active Adventure, a local company who take tourists onto the glacier, for the experience on either a snow cat or skidoo. We quickly put up our tents, de-skinned our skis and sorted our overnight bag out while enjoying the wonderful mountainous scenery.

At 1900 hours, the team all congregated into 1 tent and set upon melting snow to boil and then pour into our dried food, provided by First Expeditions food. Our first meals certainly received the thumbs up from everyone. Due to the calories burnt while traveling on the glacier, we supplemented our dried food with Pemmikan. We found it took our digestive systems several days to accustom itself to breaking down this mixture but the calories provided, will certainly benefit the team while burning the 9000 plus calories a day while down south. A quiet evening discussing our plan was enjoyed, with everyone bedding down at 2200 hours.

Mileage: 7 miles in great conditions.
Weather: Heavy snow until dropped off by Chan and Jake, then clear skies and very little wind.

Tuesday 25 Apr 06

After an amazingly quiet night, with the team having a great sleep, we arose at 0700 hours to clear skies and superb views. Utilising the conditions, we set up the cooker outside, allowing us to establish a great work routine and strike camp quickly. After sampling our first porridge and raisins and with flasks full, we started the day with a gentle descent to reach our access point to the glacier.

In near perfect conditions the route soon started to rise while we hand railed a majestic set of mountains by 2 miles ensuring to remain clear of any crevasses. We continued our climb up to the 1000 metre contour, where we were met with an incredible sight of 10 swans flying West against a clear blue sky. Under normal circumstances this wouldn't strike a chord but up here where there is minimal life, we savored the moment.

Unfortunately this was soon followed by 10 skidoos racing up the mountain, using our tracks. The noise and smell took away the feeling of at one with the environment, but after only 5 minutes they had disappeared, leaving us the last hour of ascent to enjoy this incredible scenery once more.

On stopping, we immediately set the tents up as we could see the weather changing in the distance. Within the hour we spent chilling out before cooking our food, the wind picked up to around 30 kts and the sun was engulfed by cloud, drastically dropping the temperature. I could almost see Ken's smiling face again as he handed me the 7 day forecast. Climbing into one tent again, we sampled more dried food, supplemented this time with chilli pemmikan, which tasted better. The day's sun had given a couple of troops the first signs of sunstroke, but after lots of hot and cold drink, both guys recovered quickly. After swapping a few stories, everyone braved the elements to take a very cold wee, then climbed back into their warm sleeping bags, while the unrelenting wind hammered the tents outside.

Mileage: 6.8 miles, all up hill. Very conscious of building a good foundation for the muscles in use as we still have 8 days to go.
Weather: Excellent until 1700 hours, then strong winds.

Wednesday 26 Apr 06

A very windy night, easing around 0400 hours was followed by heavy snow. The small sponge ear defenders were an essential item, so apart from a few moments I slept through the whole wind experience. With 5 inches of snow falling overnight, having laid out our basecamp in an organised manner, reaped many benefits, *i.e. you knew where your pulks and equipment was hidden!*

Fitting four of us into one tent for our meals is tight but comfy. Our admin must be kept sharp as keeping the snow outside and organising the cooking area is essential to prevent accidents. With the tents heavily ladened with snow outside, you may think it insulates the tent; it does but it also creates a lot of condensation which needs regularly mopping up.

After a slightly delayed start, at 0910 hours we headed out directly into the wind and in virtual whiteout conditions. The first hour had some downhill stretches but obviously the ascent soon started again, but fortunately it was not as steep as yesterday. We've proved that leading alternatively 1-hour stretches with a 6 - 7 minute break was the most efficient rhythm to progress our mileage. With 4 miles achieved, Ian took the lead of his 1-hour stretch but soon hit a 60 metre slope which, with all the fresh snow was waiting to avalanche. We took our skis off, took a direct line for its peak and busted a gut to quickly escape from this potentially very dangerous area. For the first time in 5 hours we had visibility, unfortunately it only lasted for 10 mins as then we were back into thick cloud and navigating by compass bearings again. As we took on our last 1 hour leg of the day, the wind subsided, the snow eased giving us just a wee break to erect our basecamp and dig in for the night. We spent an hour, servicing and cleaning the cookers as they were both burning a lot of carbon. Keeping our cookers serviceable is critical to our survival, as without them, we have no way of melting the ice and drinking the essential 4 litres of water each, we all require each day.

During the making of our dinner, we realised that instead of boiling water every time for drinks; taking the water while it was luke warm, greatly improved our fuel efficiency and greatly increased our water intake. After an hour or 2 participating in a music quiz, we headed off to bed, content in the knowledge that our admin routine was good and that we were making the best use of all our equipment and time.

Mileage: 7.2 miles.
Weather: Very strong winds, down to 50 ft visibility and blizzards.

Thursday 27 Apr 06
Awoke to shear silence; a night of no snow or wind, I even believe it didn't freeze as our skis outside were clear of ice. Working as a great team, breakfast and packing up camp was completed in 90 mins, so we were soon on route to another great day on the glacier. We achieved our plan by heading west for 3 miles into the corner of the glacier and then headed North, which included lots more uphill pulling. At the start of leg 2, the 5" of drifted wet snow resulted with the snow balling up under our skis and pulks virtually doubling the weight due to the extra resistance that we were pulling. The only thing that came into my mind was my hours of tyre pulling back at RAF High Wycombe, as it took

all my strength to clear a route for the guys to follow. After approximately 2 miles, the surface hardened again, making it so much easier to progress. With this the guys pulled off 3 great legs, all up hill and averaged 1.5 miles an hour. The last leg before camp reverted back to deep snow again, which heavily balled up under of skis and pulks again. Additionally the last 30 mins saw the winds build up from no-where which made putting up our tents quite spicy. It is worth stating, the team had adopted a great system advised by David Hempleman-Adams of only taking half the tents down, leaving the poles in situ, which greatly speeds up the process of erecting the tents. Saying this, in 35 kt winds, it's still lots of fun.

Once inside the tents in our controlled environment, we set out our routine of punching the ground to flatten the snow into a comfortable sleepable surface and letting our feet breath as they are cocooned within our "plastic bag" vapour barriers (the shop "Next" seems to have the strongest bags, which will please Clare, as a great excuse to go shopping there). Then we'd hang our socks out to dry until dinner time, when we put them inside our clothing, next to our skin, so our body heat finishes off the drying process. Then finally lay on our sleeping bags, while drinking the last droplets of our juice. This hour also gives you time to reflect on what you have achieved that day, making you realise that your efforts are so worthwhile.

Dinner tonight was supplemented with onion pemmican which appears to have received the most votes. First Expedition foods certainly have provided us with an excellent variety of tasty food, which we will definitely use again. After eating we had our second quiz, this time on First Aid and anatomy, which Mike won once again. I wonder if the fact, he was the last to leave school has any reflection on his knowledge.

Mileage: 8.2 miles.
Weather: Overcast all day, with light snow and winds. Until 1700 hours when the wind picked up again.

Friday 28 Apr 06
Very windy night, keeping the temperature down below –15 degrees all night. After eating our breakfast of porridge and raisins, we quickly took the

tents down, as once outside the shelter of the tent; your body temperature dramatically drops, hence ensuring that you are correctly dressed before stepping out into the arctic environment. However, the one main perk of such low temperatures is, it makes the surface excellent to ski on. Our first 4 legs cached in on great leads, achieving 1.7 miles per leg up hill. As the sun's heat was burning upon us, it eventually melted the top layer of snow making our last 2 legs, a lot harder. Also no sooner did we enter the soft snow, the weather once again took a turn for the worse, with visibility down to 30 ft and the winds picked up to around 30 kts. As we pulled up to our camp for the night, which was only a few metres down from the highest accessible point of the Langjokull glacier, I realised that the wind was gathering in strength by the minute. The team having put the tents up in strong winds previously very efficiently got everything sorted with 20 mins of stopping.

After taking an hours rest, the troops met in one tent and enjoyed another evening of various dried food, this time supplemented with an onion pemmikan, which once again was received very gratefully. As we had travelled over 9 miles today, we emphasised on rehydrating by drinking lots of Peminan which is another vitamin supplement hidden by either vanilla or chocolate flavour. The evening was taken up with Mikes "Trivial Pursuit" questions.

As I nipped out for a last minute wee, the wind had not eased at all and had actually averaged at around 30 plus kts gusting 50 kts.

Mileage: 9.4 miles.
Weather: Strong winds and poor visibility.

Saturday 29 Apr 06
I woke up around 0400 hours with the tent being hammered by the continual wind. According to Mike, who had not been wearing ear plugs, said it had been like this all night. As it was already light outside, you could see the wind had drifted around 8" of snow outside the tents. At 0700 hours our normal time to get up, I tried shouting across to the other tent to "stay in bed for 2 hours, to see if the wind would ease at all". I found out later they heard 2 hours and just rolled over; the wind was that strong, even my loud mouth couldn't be heard only 7 feet away.

At 0900 hours I ventured outside to witness the carnage that had happened throughout the night. The wind and ice had welded the tents to the ground, with up to 15 inches of drifting snow up the sides of the tents, the weight of which was almost collapsing the tents. The pulks, which were acting as anchor points, were completely out of sight and completely buried.

I dug my way into Pita and Ian's tent to discuss the way forward, which quickly concluded by deciding to sit out the storm and dig out the tents in a rota every 2 hours. At 1300 hours, Mike and I went outside and repositioned some of our skis to support our anchor points and dig out our disappearing tents. At 1330 hours, I phoned the Icelandic metrological office to check out the forecast for the next 12 hours; the conversation went something like this:

"Hello, could you give me the forecast for the next 12 hours for the Langjokull glacier area."

"Yes Sir, where are you now?"

"I am a team of 4 at 1320 metres up on the highest accessible point of the Langjokull glacier".

"Aaahhh that's not good, do you need help?"

"No thank you just the weather forecast please!!"

"Oh the winds will ease in the next 4 to 6 hours and should be OK tomorrow."

"Many thanks, that's great news."

"Are you sure you don't want help, that is not a good place to be?"

"No I'm certain thank you."

What was interesting and slightly disappointing was there was a muttering from a couple of the team questioning if we should had ventured to this location in the first place. My reply was simple and honest, if we're unable to handle a bit of wind here in Iceland, which is 8 hours away from safety, what chance do we have in Antarctica. The conversation was immediately dropped as I feel the person felt a little embarrassed.

This did leave me with the memorable story of Michael Fish our TV met man a decade ago, who stressed that the UK would be safe from the strong winds coming in from the West; 12 hours later the UK was hammered with hurricane winds ripping half the country apart in its aftermath!!!

Well as you can imagine, our morale took a 180 degree turn and we then enjoyed a few hours of sleep in our bags before getting the team together for an evening meal and another game of Trivial Pursuit. At around 2000 hours the wind noticeably subsided, so with a final digging out session, the troops returned to their tents for a peaceful night's sleep.

Mileage: Nil.
Weather: Up to 50 mph plus winds, heavy snow and freezing wind chill factors.

Sunday 30 Apr 06

I awoke at 0700 hours, to snow gently tapping against the tent, although this only lasted an hour. With so much deep compact frozen snow to clear, Pita cooked outside while we dug out the pulks and tents. With at least 15 inches of frozen snow to clear it took over 2 hours to clear the carnage. The only casualty of the whole night was the tent, the sewn in ground sheet had separated from the base layer leaving a gaping hole in the tent. This had been caused by weight of the snow, having frozen and built up over the nights snow fall. This had actually acted as a wind break. This irreparable damage would leave us with a wee problem to solve as we need the tent for the next 4 nights.

Due to losing a day we headed off back to our second day way point as we knew that this was a safe exit off the glacier, avoiding all crevasses as now everything was completely covered with fresh snow. The conditions with the top layer of snow gone were perfect, leaving us with the best conditions we had experienced throughout the trip, especially with pulling our pulks. We headed basically south and covered over 10 miles on perfect snow in whiteout conditions.

As we reached our camp, it gently snowed but without the wind, this made erecting the tents a lot easier than previous days. The torn tent was resolved by placing 2 pulks at an angle as a wind break, packing the gaps full of snow and placing rucksacks on the inside for support.

The main reason for navigating back to our location was that we presumed that the position 56th RQS had dropped us off at would be completely blocked with drifted snow, hence we would probably have to ski back a further 20 miles to reach an accessible point, which would be our way of helping the guys who had been so helpful to us. At around 1900 hours Pita and I went over to the other tent for our meal and to discuss our exit plan. We all enjoyed another quiz which this time Ian won by at least 6 points.

Mileage: 10.3 miles.
Weather: Little snow fall, white out conditions, light winds.

Monday 1 May 06

I awoke around 0600 hours to shear silence, so I spent the next hour contemplating our 2 trips to Iceland and realised that these expeditions will be one of the many keys to our success with our quest for the South Pole. I was pondering about who could take over as Expedition Leader. With Kirky in Iraq and Phil and Kev being unavailable to join us due to work commitments I had not gained a warm confident feeling about the 3 guys I was out here with to take over my lead. The decision was silently tearing me apart.

At 0700 hours we got up to magnificent views, so quickly decided to cook breakfast outside. After striking camp and enjoying our breakfast, we started our descent to the mountain hut. Within minutes the clouds engulfed us dropping the visibility to 50 ft; 2 ½ miles later we picked up the skidoo tracks, which lead us back to the hut. After a 10 minute break, we headed further south, heading back to the point where the track met the road. To our astonishment, the access road was clear, with 4 x 4 wagons driving along it with caution. We immediately sparked up the Iridium satellite phone to speak to Ken Howk, to ascertain if his troops could pick us up tomorrow. After chatting to Ken, we were told to "wait out" to confirm his decision as meetings were being held that afternoon to decide on the closure timings of their station for his troops.

We decided to put up our tents in a sheltered place and set up for what could be 2 days of waiting. At 1800 hours I phoned Ken, who gave us the great news that his troops would leave first thing tomorrow and should be with us at 0830 hours tomorrow, at the junction which is only 1 km away. We sparked the cooker up and had dinner earlier than usual, as we would have an early start tomorrow. Knowing that we had extra fuel, we all enjoyed lots of juice and hot chocolate drinks. At 2100 hours we bedded down and enjoyed a great night's sleep.

Mileage: 9 miles.
Weather: Light winds, poor visibility, good skiing conditions.

Tuesday 2 May 06

Arising at 0600 hours, we skipped breakfast until later, struck camp and enjoyed a great ski down to the road junction. On arrival of the junction, we sparked up the cooker and enjoyed a brew and our belated breakfast. As the wind blew through the glen, we hid behind a huge pile of stones for shelter until around 1000 hours, when I phoned Ken to ask for a situation report on the troops on route. I was advised that the guys had been approximately 3 miles away from our pick up point and due to drifted snow, which we could not have envisaged from our current location, were heading back to Keflavik. After several more calls, we moved down, skiing through the patches of snow to the point where the guys reached and were delighted to hear that the guys would try again later on today.

We erected the tent to shelter from the wind for 3 hours and then carried our pulks for approximately a mile as the patchy snow had taken us away from the track. With excellent views, we saw the 2 wagons on route from over 2 miles away. The time it took the wagons to pick us up, gave me time to quickly reflect that our trip on the glacier was over and that we had achieved all our training objectives and more.

As the guys arrived, we quickly loaded up the pulks into the wagons and jumped into a warm, comfy and inviting seat, which felt like heaven compared to the crunched up roll mats and spongy sleeping bag we had been accustomed to for the past week.

A 3 hour drive and we were back at Keflavik; we immediately unloaded all of our equipment into the section, hanging up our tents and laying out all our gear to air overnight. Showing the full extent of the damaged caused to the tent we had borrowed, brought a few interesting comments on just how bad had the weather been up there. Well by the time the troops had showered and got around to Eric Barry's room we all shared a couple of beers, while the winds on the base were blasting up to 80 mph creating 20 inches of drifted snow. As for the temperatures, who knows, but I'm sure in beers and stories to come, the wind speeds and temperatures will deteriorate further.

Wednesday 3 May 06

Incredibly the troops did not sleep too well, considering they were in a warm billet and between clean sheets of a comfy bed. Anyway we met up for breakfast in the Chow hall and basically ate for Britain to recuperate some of the calories that we had lost over the past 10 days. With full stomachs, we walked around to the section, to start packing our equipment away, as we were very conscious that the USAF detachment in Iceland was coming to a very quick conclusion and that our kit spread out all over their section would only hinder there packing. As we packed our equipment, it came apparent that we had taken the exact amount of equipment needed and no more. Having the food, fuel, crevasse rescue kit, waterproofs and overnight equipment all sealed in separate bags had worked very well, as none of our equipment had got wet, hence saving valuable weight.

Incredibly it took over 3 hours to repack our equipment, so following lunch we hired a car from on base and treated ourselves to a dip in the Blue Lagoon, one of the world's largest natural heated water baths. Even though the guys had not encountered many muscle problems, this was a perfect remedy to wash away any small aches or pains.

Utilising the car, we took Ken, Eric and Chris into Reykjavik (which is an incredibly large city) for an evening meal. The csot of living in iceland is extremely high. To give you an example the cost of hiring a 7 seater van for just 24 hours would have cost £309, so hiring from base was great value! An excellent evening was enjoyed by all, with the Icelandic Sushi house providing us with wonderful food.

Thursday 4 May 06

A 0515 hours start for Mike and I, as Mike had to return a day early for a medical appointment. Once happy that Mike had not incurred any excess baggage charges, I headed back to our billet to catch another couple of hours sleep. Following breakfast, the 3 of us headed into Keflavik, to only confirm that there actually is nothing there, so we returned back to base to help the 56 RQS guys pack up the rescue equipment and help them to move some equipment from the their section to a secure lock up. This seemed to be the minimum that we could do for these guys who had supported so well.

That evening, the troops met up with the 56th RQS guys in the local bar, where the team presented expedition tee shirts to the guys and a few bottles of Malt whisky to be shared at their forthcoming closure party.

Friday 5 May 06

Another 0515 hours start this time for all of us, as Ken arrived at 0530 hours sharp to take us on the short journey to the airport. Saying our farewells to Ken was a humorous occasion as we knew that it would only be 1 week later that Ken would be taking his own truck from Iceland via ferry to Aberdeen and then driving down to Lakenheath via Edinburgh, where Ian and Mike would host him for an evening in one of Scotland's most glorious cities. After bartering with the airhostess at Icelandic Air, we brought the cost down of our excess baggage, which compared to our previous expedition saved us a fortune. Another uneventful flight brought us back into T2 Heathrow airport, where we unpacked all of our equipment, which had been borrowed from Bicester and then carefully moved it around to T1 where High Wycombe MT were ready to pick me and all the equipment up. Why not T2 you may ask, yes so did I? The answer was simple, driver was told to go to T1, even though my request was T2, to pick up an officer and we would have to move. He wasn't even an executive, so much for common sense, or for someone with a back bone!! A quick farewell was said and that was it, Exercise Atlantic Ice was over. We had set out with a huge criterion of tests and plans, we had achieved them all and more and we knew that with a few tweaks here and there, our quest to lead the Royal Air Force to the South Pole was now becoming a reality.

Camping on the Vatnajokull Glacier, Iceland.

Camping on the Langjokull Glacier in 50mph winds, heavy snow and freezing wind chill factors. *"That's not a good place to be"* according to the weather people!

Chapter 5
Phase 3: May 2006 - August 2006

May 2006

Following the success of our second expedition, the next couple of weeks were all about communications. I now needed to ensure that all the agencies involved, senior officers and potential sponsors, knew that the team had performed admirably with our new equipment but we had one major ingredient missing, money! This very time consuming effort conflicted with my primary work within communications, but once again the COMSEC team covered for me in so many ways that I managed to see everyone within that fortnight. The feedback and overall feeling I received was positive but no one was in a position to authorise me any additional money.

The 2 most important interviews were with the HQAT who were very keen to enquire how well the team was gelling together, how was their fitness improving and what problems was I struggling from? We had a great catch up but I couldn't help feel during our chat that there was still an underground swell of disbelief that the expedition may still not happen. Being on my own during these interviews is where I had to dig exceptionally deep to maintain my positive attitude and belief as I was being hit with such negative vibes from so many directions. I guess I can only compare it to a boxer with a cut above the eye, pleading with the referee to let them fight on. As apart from a little cut, the boxer is still a lean mean fighting machine. Regardless of the cutting comments, I wasn't going to let them stop living this dream.

The other interviews were with the RAF Senior Leadership Team and the 3 officers who were the heads of finance, logistics and catering. Again, once the niceties of how and what had happened in Iceland was answered, the main subject was finance. Although there was a certain amount of flex that could be re-molded, the astronomical money I needed to pay to be flown on the ice from Chile, have daily communications coverage and the flight back from the bottom of the earth didn't fall under any of their remits. The total invoice to be paid to Antarctic Logistics & Expeditions (ALE) was £124,500. You may be reading in astonishment, so was I was when I first received the draft invoice. But the main expenditure was the flight back from the South Pole back to the Patriot Hills. Remembering this was ground breaking adventure for the RAF, the thought of skiing unsupported for 600 nautical miles was one thing but reciprocating our route under our own steam was out of the question. The other concrete fact was that ALE had the franchise, no one else could fly us out from Chile, and so we either pay up or gave up.

Following the meetings, I spoke to the team giving them all the feedback I had received, which on the whole was positive but with the one negative aspect. From this the guys came up with several ideas, which I left them to follow with the instruction to put their heart on their sleeve when approaching the company. The only hook we had was to advertise their product on our clothing and sledges, which isn't a lot when we were asking for around £10K per donation. Then came the fantastic news that Kev Eaton at RAF Cranwell had managed to source £15K to be utilised for promoting the team on TV, radio and local newspaper, all in the name of recruiting for the RAF. This was another perfect hook to obtain more sponsors. As the Central Office of Information (COI) was based in London, it provided a great opportunity for the guys to meet the COI, see what they could do and follow it up with a second visit to the FCO.

Prior to meeting the COI, the team threw lots of ideas into the mix, like appearing on Blue Peter, Sky Sports programs, cookery programs to use pemmikan, BBC Radio 5 live, local BBC stations and newspapers from where we originated from and other children's programs. So as I met with the COI guys in London, I was immediately deflated when they agreed they were all great ideas and the troops should go ahead and arrange them; what was the RAF paying them for? They wanted snippets of what we were planning and then they may possibly add it into the RAF's major advertising campaign. I was gutted and left their building frustrated but I felt this gave us the carte blanche green light to advertise our quest via any means. The only problem was we are RAF troops, how with all the other work going on, do we establish comms with all these agencies. Over the coming months we managed several radio and local paper interviews but the big advertising on the major programs never materialised. As a note, you may want to compare our quest with the publicity our fellow Army and Royal Navy colleagues receive when they attempt high profile adventurous challenges, the RAF really do let themselves down in this area.

The day wasn't a total loss, as the visit to see David at the FCO again was a resounding success as he had approved our expedition and we were given the blessing from the highest authorities in the FCO. This was a joker card certificate to take back to RAF Command as now our expedition had even more emphasis to go ahead.

Back on the financial front, we were starting to have some success with some major companies, all of who had a direct link with the RAF. Companies like QinetiQ, Babcock's and Austin Heyes all came on board, which was perfect as we now had to start thinking about communications from Antarctica. As the good news came in regarding the money, Kev Eaton phoned me regarding his position within my team. I humbly recognised Kev had been working flat out trying to co-ordinate the teams' funds which was starting to encroach on his work life balance. After a very long conversation, Kev decided to withdraw his position as a contender to head to south, but was adamant that he wanted to continue supporting the team in any other way he could. Although secretly devastated with Kev's news, I fully respected his decision and was incredibly grateful for his wish to continue helping me.

June 2006
What we needed from our communications was something light, simple and as cheap as possible to send messages and photos back from Antarctica to a website hosted in the UK. With Kirky just back from Iraq and he was our techno man, he volunteered to research what previous expeditions had used and then try and find the latest technology for 2006. One mandatory requirement we had to fulfil was while on the ice, we must check in with ALE every day with a situation report. To ensure this, we needed to obtain

2 Nokia Satellite phones. The first phone was borrowed for free from the RAF's Tactical Communications Wing, the 2nd Kev Eaton managed to hire with 3000 minutes of coverage on it, paid for by the recruiting team; step one complete. This is where Kirky came into his element, but sourcing a Personal Digital Assistant (PDA), basically a small computer the size of your hand that could process pictures and a daily written update. Now Kirky had to trial, test and bang his head against a brick wall, trying to get the phone and PDA to talk to each other, in came the Compact 3 software to marry the comms. At the same time, a wonderful guy called Chris Toms, a civil servant based at RAF High Wycombe had volunteered to build the expedition a website that could not only communicate with the PDA but also require no other human intervention to work. Writing this in 1 paragraph, now makes me smile, as the time and effort Kirky and Chris put it to get the comms package working took over 2 months, I can only take my hat off to them both.

Also in June, I was requested by HQAT to provide an update on the progress being made on both the planning for our final training expedition to Norway and the South Pole. Previously, I had simply collected all my files and folders and casually walked in and just delivered a brief, but something suspicious sparked inside me, so this time I prepared a power point presentation. As I walked into the briefing room, there was not only the 3 HQAT team but their boss plus 2 other people who I didn't recognise. The 2 guys were from the Royal Marines, Major Sean Chappel (Expedition Leader) and a fellow Antarctic team member, who were also planning on going to the South Pole at the same time, via a different route. I was furious, absolutely raging as although I knew about Sean's team and their intentions, I felt HQAT had purposely arranged the meeting to catch me out. Sean's team had already successfully reached the North Pole earlier in the year and was now in the final planning stages for the South. Once introduced, I internally calmed down and set about providing a presentation on our achievements and our final plans. As the various areas were covered, I invited questions, which opened the HQAT door to compare what Sean was doing in comparison. For me, standing at the front answering the questions, felt like a lamb waiting to be slaughtered. Then came the "Halleluiah" moment when Sean who with his previous North and South Pole experience, announced that his planning was very similar and that I had stringently planned our expedition down to the finest detail and that he looked forward to seeing us in Chile. Even though, I knew I still needed to raise thousands of pounds, I felt the world had fallen off my shoulders. This to me also said that HQAT could now authorise the expedition, which a few days later, they finally did.

The big difference between Sean's expedition was his team of 4 were planning to kite ski back from the South Pole, hence saving £1000's. With a lot lighter atmosphere in the room, Sean went on to highlight that he and several members of his team had been authorised to stand down from their primary duties so that he could concentrate on the expedition. I looked for a reaction from HQAT as I was working flat out 16 hours a day, apart from 1 raised eye brow, not a word was spoken. Like the publicity, in my experience the expedition leaders from the Army, Royal Navy and Royal Marines are all given the time to co-ordinate these huge expeditions, this is another area, where the RAF may want to give due consideration for future trips. Sean and I swapped details, which I followed up by visiting him at the Commando Training Centre at Lympstone a few weeks later. Sean had his own office and a small area to store all his expedition equipment. I met 2 other members of his team and we all sat over lunch chatting and comparing our plans for November. Although we clearly had different plans our overall objective of reaching the bottom of our planet was magnetic with all our discussions being spoken about so enthusiastically. I came away from my visit very humbled as Sean's team were highly impressed with our planning and training as the unwritten belief is the RAF don't do such adventurous expeditions as our fellow Armed Forces colleagues. I personally don't agree with the RAF MRS summiting Mt Everest and the previous expeditions in the 1980's and 90's to Antarctic's Smith and Baffin Island prove otherwise.

Meanwhile back in Phil's world of logistics, he had spent hours researching sleeping bags, tents and wolverine fur for our gortex jackets. Once again there was a huge disparity of what could be provided by our Army colleagues at Bicester and what we actually needed. The sleeping bags that were routinely distributed to all the troops were not adequate and had not been tested down to -40 degrees, which was essential. So Phil had found a synthetic and down filled Mountain Equipment sleeping bag that fulfilled all our requirements. The next item was a tent. Historically the Terra Nova Mountain Quasar was the tent of choice as it had been used on Mt Everest and various high altitude expeditions. What was screaming out from Phil's research was a Swedish company called Hilleberg, was what virtually every Antarctic expedition was using including Sean's team. Hilleberg tents instead of being the geodesic domed shape were more a tunnel shaped tent to deflect the wind more efficiently, which is key when this is your only shelter. My only reply to Phil was to say yes and then cringe at how much money he needed. The 4 sleeping bags were £400 each and the tents £750 each and we needed 2! Thankfully Sir Brian's letter to the Station Commanders was starting to build some capital in our bank but as this kit was essential for our safety, I gave Phil the go ahead to purchase them. Once again Phil followed this with his captivating laugh by saying "oops I've forgot, I also need another £400 for the wolverine fur for our gortex jackets" as this needs to be imported from the USA. This may seem a little extravagant but the reason why the fur is needed is to create a warm environment within the hooded area of the jacket. The best way to describe how it works is to compare it with when you walk into a large shop. Once the automatic shop doors open, you are met with a heater above you pushing heat onto your head. What this does, it stops the cold air coming into the shop and hence reducing the shop's heating bill. Wolverine fur creates virtually the same affect. You pull the fur around your googles creating a warm environment inside the shell of your hood so you can breathe relatively warm air in, hence maintaining your body temperature. So why you see people walking down the High Street of your main shopping area wearing a fur covered hood in the local town or city is beyond me!

You may be wondering what was happening on my domestic front with Clare being pregnant and me withdrawing as expedition leader. Well, within a couple of weeks of returning from Iceland, I came home from work one evening to find all of my files and folders spread out over the living room floor. As I had become quite attached to my work, I looked at Clare and apprehensively questioned what was happening. I'm unable to write how my heart felt when Clare replied, that in front of me was 2 years of my life, 2 years of misplaced heart beats, 2 years of sleepless nights and 2 years of putting together one of the RAF most important expeditions in years. I stood in silence, which for me is rare and then replied with the tears running down my face that I still had my moral responsibilities as a father to our unborn child. Clare stood with my work strewn out between us and said *"why put aside all this effort to what has been your dream for so long, for our baby that will be here for when you return, also I don't want to be responsible for you having any regrets?"* I was left speechless only for the silence to be broken with our front door bell ringing.

Breaking the atmosphere, I quickly dried my eyes as I walked slowly to answer the door, only to find Clare's Mum and Dad stood with their huge smiles stood in the doorway. With huge hugs and welcoming gestures completed, John walks into the living room, see's all the folders over the floor and quotes "what's all this about you not trusting us to look after our daughter and grandchild while you're away on your expedition". For the 3rd time in less than 5 minutes I was left speechless. Should I argue, should I upset everyone, or should I listen and follow my dream? There is no doubt that with every expedition I have been on, there is an element of selfishness and definitely arrogance, but they are 2 of the ingredients that give you the passion to strive for success. I had left loved ones behind on previous expeditions but an unborn baby? The conversation with Clare, Ann and John went on for a while, but concluded with my brain completely mangled, my heart torn into 3 and the conclusion that I would go to Antarctica. This roller coaster of emotions just kept going on and on and on.

Something else I was keen to involve with the expedition was my old secondary school based in Grimsby. Incredibly my physical education teacher Geoff Todd was still teaching at Havelock, so together we tied up our diaries so that I could provide a presentation to the school. It also provided the opportunity for my family and friends to join us for the presentations, one of which was Dave Emberson, who I had not seen for many years. Dave and my friendship go back over 30 years as we had served in the 11th Grimsby Scouts together. Having not visited him for decades, I was surprised to see very little had changed apart from we were all a little older. Geoff arranged for 2 presentations so every pupil had the opportunity to ask questions and hopefully inspire them to go on to achieve great things in their future. It was very humbling attending my old school, especially when I returned back to High Wycombe, to receive a cheque for £618, which had been raised during a dress down day, which the pupils had requested that it was donated to my expedition. Although it had not been my intention, the visit to Grimsby had generated almost a £1000 in donations from my school, Dave and his parents and my niece's school who also kindly donated after providing them a presentation too. At last, everything coming together, the expedition was becoming a family of agencies willing us to succeed.

30 June

It wasn't just the amazing donations of money being received. When Clare and I shared a fantastic day with over 100 other guests at Bob and Bev Ballinger's wedding, we sat listening to Bob's traditional after dinner speech where he thanked everyone for coming and for all their kind presents. Just as he was about to conclude his heartfelt comments, he stopped and diverted this special moment in time speech to wish me and my team "God Speed" with our forthcoming expedition. The whole room proudly and loudly applauded and then cheered. This left me feeling so humbled, honoured and tearful as for the first time; I now knew how other people felt about our adventure and how serious people were taking us.

The final task I had before departing for Norway was to put in place a date and venue for our farewell function for all our sponsors, senior leadership, supporters and families. As with all big expeditions it gives the team great pleasure to bring together all of the agencies and main characters that have helped to produce the final product of seeing the team together before departing for their mammoth challenge. Realising the Officers' Mess at RAF High Wycombe has a wonderful historic mansion housed set within beautiful gardens, I asked the Station Commander for her permission to hold the function there, to which she was only too happy to host. So the scene was set, we had the equipment, we had the high level support, I had 5 highly motivated guys that I had to reduce to 3 and find a mere £50K before September. I mean, what could go wrong?

Chapter 6
Exercise Northern Lights

RAF Norway Expedition, 5 August - 13 August 2006

Again this part of the book is a redacted version of the official post expedition report from our third and final training expedition.

The aim, objectives, support and finances were the same as the planning for Exercise Cold Feet and Atlantic Ice, the only thing different was the equipment, as now we had now purchased all of our own equipment.

Nominal Roll
The following personnel participated in Exercise Northern Lights:

- WO A Sylvester, *Headquarters Strike Command, High Wycombe*
- Sgt I Stewart, *RAF Leuchars*
- Cpl I Kirk, *RAF Kinloss*
- Cpl, M Beveridge, *RAF Leuchars*
- Cpl P Mainprize, *RAF Halton*
- Pita, *RAF*

The diary below gives a detailed personal account of the events that took place during Exercise Northern Lights.

2/3/4 Aug 06
Utilising an idea by Mike and Ian while organising Exercise Norwegian Light, they volunteered to drive down from RAF Leuchars in Fife to RAF Halton in Buckinghamshire to transport the equipment over to Norway by road and ferry rather than via air which would have incurred horrendous excess baggage fees. So after picking the wagon from their vehicle centre, their first mammoth

journey was to drive down to Halton to pick up the equipment already owned by the team and borrowed from the Army at Bicester.

With 4 of us securing the kit into the wagon we soon finished the packing and headed for a quick beer before the guys headed off at 0600 hours the following morning, heading back up to Newcastle. The guys arrived at Newcastle with plenty of time before their overnight ferry crossing to Kristiansand, which landed on Friday morning leaving them a 6 hour drive to Oslo, where they stayed in a hostel overnight awaiting our arrival the following day.

Saturday 5 Aug 06

Ian and Mike were joined very early in the morning by Phil who had arranged an earlier flight as he had co-ordinated a great money saving deal with Sportsnett.no. Here they picked up lots of specialist cold weather equipment before the arrival of the remainder of the team. With everyone in Oslo by 1800 hours, we immediately headed North towards Juuvashytta were, on arrival we found the park gates closed so we forced to move back down the valley to a forest where the guys slept in their bivvy bags with a great view of the stars and passing satellites.

Sunday 6 Aug 06

A great night's sleep was had by all, so utilising the space around us the team sorted out their equipment for our next few days on the ice. After a quick breakfast, we successfully got through the gate, paying our £10 road fees to allow us to reach the snout of the glacier. It was here after lifting our jaws off the floor, we were greeted to a glacier that could only be described as crevasse or death city. After talking to a couple of local guides we were informed that for first time in Norway's history, all the snow slopes had been forced to close due to the rising temperatures. The owner of the ski centre verified the situation after having closed the resort only 3 days prior to arrival. This was small a consolation considering we had checked out the websites only 7 days previously. Although completed disheartened we made the most of the day by walking to the side of the glacier where we carried out the various crevasse rescue techniques that we may need to utilise during our intrepid voyage. Once back at the wagon we used the great back drop to interview the team as part of our footage requested by the RAF Corporate Communications team, who had agreed to edit our footage and build a documentary on our expedition. Returning back to the forest in the early evening, we enjoyed an al fresco meal (dried food, just add boiling water), surrounded by the magnificent barely snow capped mountains, followed by the team working together to plan a walking/mountaineering route instead.

As expeditions take you away from the normal routines of modern day life, part of our trials during our visit to Norway was to establish our link back to Chris Toms our website manager back at RAF High Wycombe. This link will be essential during our expedition, to keep everyone informed of our daily progress. Well after much "twoing and froing", we managed to send back an email via the Iridium satellite phone link. Although successful, the amount of time used up on the net at £2 a minute, took too long, so this link is going to have to be investigated further. The second technical test, involved setting off our emergency beacon kindly provided by HR Smith. This emergency beacon, once sparked, sends a signal to various Mission Control Centre's around the world including RAF Kinloss. With the assistance of Tom Taylor MBE, a retired RAF Mountain Rescue team leader based at Kinloss, we successfully achieved all our tasks proving that this beacon can be used as our last ditch communications in the event of an emergency in the south.

Even though the skiing aspect of the expedition has been dissolved, the team planned to utilise the week to build their mountain fitness and build upon their team spirit, which will undoubtedly be one of the keys to our success in reaching the South Pole.

Weather: Hot and sunny, with no wind

Monday 7 Aug 06
The troops were awoken at around 03:45 hours with the sound of torrential rain battering the outsides of our bivvy bags. As at 0345 hours it was already clear daylight, we could see that this was not just a passing storm, so everyone tightened the hood on their bivvy bags and slept through to 0700 hours. As it was still raining, we descended back to the wagon where we enjoyed breakfast (porridge with raisins), followed by heading back to Lom (small village 15

kms away) so the guys could purchase a few items to help them with their forthcoming 3 day walking expedition. After confirming with the tourist information that the weather was to improve, we headed up another valley to a campsite called Spiterstulen. On arrival we packed up a day sack and headed off further up the valley to ascend up 1200 metres up to the Svellnosbreen glacier, where several parties were practicing glacier travel while dodging the array of crevasses. After a wee photo session, the team descended down to our camp for the night where we once again enjoyed the culinary delights of the various menus provided by First Choice Expedition foods. To ensure we attain all the calories we require down south all our meals are supplemented with Pemmikan. With 2 of the team having not tasted this culinary delight before, it was with great amusement, we watched the disgust in their faces as they tasted it for the first time. After dinner we tried another internet link, but after several attempts I reverted to phoning Chris with our daily update for our website. This maybe our only option to keep the costs down, the only down side is we are unable to send back photo's.

After a wee team meeting we finalised the plan for the next 3 days, followed by chilling out in the communal campsite building, where we spent the rest of the evening.

Weather: Heavy rain in the morning, but fortunately cleared in the afternoon.

Tuesday 8 Aug 06

After an early start, the team finalised their packing for our multi day trip and set off into the heart of the glen that we had seen from a distance for the past 2 days. Our first hours hand railed a glacial river, providing us some sporty jumps and leaps over some little streams crossing our way ahead. As per our last training expedition to Iceland, each troop led an hour at a time, allowing 10 mins per break, to give us the feeling of the timings that we will echo in the south. As the sun beamed down on us, most troops striped down to a pair of shorts, carefully covering themselves in sun cream. Also we maintained a disciplined pace trying hard not to sweat too much.

3 hours, 12kms and 1000 metres into our day's route, we took an extended break, to jump into a glacial loch. Although the majority of photos will remain

under lock and key, the guys plunged into the freezing waters, for around 20 seconds before parts of our anatomy started to disappear. After defrosting in the sun and scaring the passing solo walker, we put back on our now dried freshly baked clothes and carried on with our route.

Having only seen 1 person all day, to our surprise we passed a group of around 20 walkers of different origin, after a wee chat, we started our descent towards a superb glacial loch, where our bivvy site lay ahead. Ensuring that we had running water, a flat/dry sleeping area, sheltered from the wind, space for our 3 tents, we established an excellent site, once again with breath taking views. Once the camp was established, the troops took an hour to sort out their personal admin, followed by a brew and sending back our daily update to Chris. Also we sparked our emergency beacon again, once again achieving great results, which is very reassuring.

The remainder of the evening was spent adding to our list of final equipment that we will use down south. We also sneaked in several games of X Men top trumps; it's amazing what simple things can keep the troops occupied. As the sun dropped behind the mountains, the temperature naturally dropped so everyone sank into the warmth of their sleeping bags for a great night's sleep.

Weather: Warm and sunny with light winds

Wednesday 9 Aug 06

Awaking at around 0630 hours to cracking views, the troops enjoyed another al-fresco breakfast and continued with the route in glorious weather. As the maps were marginal at best, to our surprise within a couple of hours we came across another mountain bothy, selling teas and coffees, which was a very welcome break. After this great morale boost, we headed off circumnavigating a large loch, which brought us back to our planned route. Unfortunately the weather took a turn for the worse and proceeded to test our gortex jackets. As our route over the past 2 days had been surrounded by the edges of various glaciers, no sooner did the rain start, the water rushed off the glaciers, raising the river water levels to raging torrents. Although blessed with several bridges, the team enjoyed utilising their poles to jump across some of the more challenging rivers that had now been produced from the glaciers above. Quite ironically as we approached our overnight campsite, the rain eased, allowing us to put the tents up in the dry, which was a bonus. Each night the team had swapped around who they shared the tent with, to keep the team mixing and give the troops time to get to know each other. As the troops sank into the sleeping bags, the rain started again, this from inside our dry tents was very therapeutic.

Weather: Lovely start but was followed with torrential rain.

Thursday 10 Aug 06

After a very wet and windy night, the rain finally stopped, providing the troops with a clear morning. After breakfast they quickly repacked their rucksacks for today's route which was to ascend Norway's highest mountain Galdhopiggen 2469 metres. The route started with an immediate steep climb for 1000 metres, which topped out with magnificent views of 2 huge glaciers, both of which beckoned us with open crevasses, which further strengthened our decision to stay off the ice. As we gained more height, with 200 metres of ascent to go, all visibility disappeared, so we ascended the final ridge with caution as we had also hit a very wet snow line. After a little over 3 ½ hours, the team reached the summit, only to find another huge group within the mountain refuge hut, who had ascended from Juuvashytta. Although we didn't take up the offer of tea or coffee, we took our photos and headed back down to the campsite. We touched base with Chris again and updated our website for the last time, as tomorrow we are heading to Lillehammer then onto Oslo to exchange some of the equipment that we had purchased earlier in the trip.

Weather: Clear for most of the day, cloudy over the summits

Friday 11 Aug 06

The morning was spent separating the equipment into expedition, personal and Bicester owned, so it would save a lot of work back at Halton. Later that morning we departed on our journey home for Lillehammer to break up the journey to Oslo.

On route we came across an Olympic bobsleigh track, so we all thoroughly enjoyed an impromptu ride at 60 mph with our bums only 2 inches above the ground. It was awesome. After returning to terra-firma we continued to

Lillehammer, where we set up our tents and humble abode for the night. A pleasant night was had by all, tasting the products from the local hostelries, which at £7.50 a pint, made some drinks hard to swallow.

Saturday 12 Aug 06

During Friday evening, I took the opportunity to talk to the troops about their feeling about each team member, which raised some concerning worries about a couple of the team. The apprehension included how well they fitted into the team, team ethos and fitness. My thoughts returned to the original requirement from HQAT which stipulated that I needed 4 people who fitted together like a hand in a glove. The troop's comments echoed my sentiments which as a leader reassured me that I was making the right decision of who I should take to the South Pole.

After striking camp and breakfast, I took a walk for 30 minutes to confirm in my mind that I was making the right decision. I felt empty in my stomach knowing I was about to ruin 2 people's dream of Antarctica, but I knew as a leader, I had to make the right choice. Having had 18 months of bonding and training the team, this was undoubtedly the hardest decision I had had to make in the whole my 2½ years of organising this major expedition.

My final decision had to leave me with no doubts or hesitation of everyone's all round ability to reach the GSP. Based on this I selected Phil Mainprize, Iain Kirk and Pita to go with me.

My announcement left the team with mixed emotions of great disappointment for Ian and Mike and feelings of happiness and sadness for the 3 other guys. The drive to Oslo was very intense and obviously a very quiet affair with everyone contemplating the announcement and assessing the final tasks that are required to complete our pre expedition plans. On arrival in Oslo, we headed back to Sjur's shop Sportsnett to exchange some equipment and collect the last few items for the main expedition. After finding and setting up camp, we headed into the centre of Oslo to check out the highlights of this wonderful city; but as our plan was to start at 0400 hours on Sunday, the guys returned back to the campsite early to get some sleep, before Sunday's journey.

Sunday 13 Aug 06

Ian and Mike dropped off the troops at their airports and headed back on their 6 hour drive back to Kristiansand where they caught their ferry for the overnighter back to Newcastle. Although some flights were delayed from Norway due to terrorist activities in the week, the troops all successfully got back to the UK by one flight or another.

Monday 14 Aug 06

To help Ian and Mike with their mammoth journey, Phil and I drove up from RAF Halton to meet them at RAF Leeming. After swapping the equipment, both wagons headed North and South respectively, concluding what had been an emotional roller coaster of an expedition. As you've just read the expedition's intention was to carry out skiing, pulk tests and living on ice for a week. Well in good RAF tradition, I believe the team made the very best from the conditions with regards to fitness, tent admin and team building. The final team selection was an exceptionally difficult decision as the guys had all worked so well together, but I had to leave myself without any hesitation of my team who will travel unsupported the 600 nautical miles to the Geographic South Pole. Ian and Mike both worked tirelessly to not only put Exercise Norwegian Light together but had also worked with the pre planning for Southern Reach. Even though there are now only 4 people attempting the South Pole, without their help the team would not have reached this far to date.

Conditions on the Juuvashytta were out of our control!

Chapter 7
Phase 4: August 2006 - November 2006

Immediately on returning from Norway, I set about announcing the team to our sponsors and senior leadership team. This time I included the Station Commander from RAF Leuchars as both Ian and Mike were serving on his station and he had financially supported us throughout our training. As a mark of respect of his support, I decided to write a personal letter explaining how and why I had my decision. The following week, I received a reply thanking me for my explanation and he wished the team the very best on our adventure.

28 Aug 2006

After 2 ½ years of stress, planning and training the next few hours were going to make or break our expedition. Having discussed the current state of our finances with Kev Eaton, I realised we only had 3 weeks before our final payment to ALE. We had prompted all our big likely sponsors and had collected over £130K but this left us £50K short. There was only 1 interview that could achieve it. So I made the call to the RAF's new Commander In Chief's (CinC) Sir Joe French outer office to book an interview. Sir Joe was not a mountaineer and I had never met him apart from passing him in the corridor, while standing to attention. To my relief, I booked an appointment that afternoon. While sitting in the waiting area, I rehearsed and rehearsed my speech and plan, and then the moment of conviction arrived as I was invited to enter his office. The first 5 minutes was very polite and welcoming as I reeled off our achievements to date, especially on the recruiting side and on how our fellow Armed Forces colleagues were in awe of the RAF's planning and intentions. Then came the guillotine stroke, as I veered the discussions direction towards finances. My stomach was in a knot; my heart felt like it was beating at my tonsils as I asked for £50K of support. He responded with a huge sigh and silence. Not sure whether he was inviting me to talk; I broke into a line I had rehearsed about how I was taking the Armed Forces adventurous training into a new ground breaking league, with the RAF at the fore. He replied with various proposals, with a conclusion that he could possibly stretch to a grant of £30K. Knowing this wasn't enough, I had to stand with conviction to argue my case, it had to be £50K or the expedition was off. As CinC he rightfully holds great authority with so many aspects of the RAF and told me that £30K was his final offer. Then totally out of the blue, I decided without any hesitation to actually fall to my knees and plead for the money. The look on Sir Joe's face and his personal assistant was of total horror. As a Warrant Officer of 24 years' service I had stooped to the depths of my knees as I explained how passionately I wanted this expedition to happen for the RAF. It was the longest 15 seconds of my life, but Sir Joe's response can only be described as heaven sent. He calmly replied, that he had witnessed many experiences in his RAF career, but that had knocked the wind out of his sails as he agreed to sign off £50K as long as I got up and returned to my chair. Within seconds the conversation was over, I saluted Sir Joe and calmly marched out of his office. As I walked back to my office I felt numb, the reality of what I had just done was incomprehensible but for the first time in 2 ½ years, I knew without any doubt, we were now going to Antarctica.

The final plans all now fell into place. With great pride I wrote the cheque from our expedition to Antarctic Logistics & Expeditions for £124K, all my worries about money was over. Chris Toms had not only designed a fantastic website but along with Kirky, together they had cracked the communications link between the PDA and our website and we could now send photos and daily updates without any human intervention.

While all this was going on Phil had been co-ordinating and finalising all our equipment and food and arranging for the team to meet up and utilise a hangar for the weekend at RAF Halton. In mid September we all met up and laid out all our food and equipment all over a vast area, wow, we had accumulated so much equipment; Phil had done an amazing job. Pairing up we filled our boxes, ensuring that each item on the list had been packed and ticked off the list, as once we were in Chile, there would be no opportunity to replace any missing items. Incredibly this took 7 hours to complete but with that much effort I was happy that everything was serviceable and ready to go. The boxes were sealed and addresses applied as Phil had arranged for them to be picked up from Halton and then despatched by sea to Punta Arenas in Chile at a cost of around £3K return.

The next time the team came together was for our leaving function at the end of September in the Officer's Mess at RAF High Wycombe. It was an honour to bring together our sponsors, Master Sergeant Ken Howk and his 56th USAF Rescue team, David Hempleman Adams, Sir Joe French and an abundance of outstanding people who had help me put this expedition together. I provided a presentation to our guests followed by a wonderful sit down meal provided by the mess. Sir Joe spoke and passed on his heartfelt wishes from the RAF, thankfully not mentioning my begging performance and Ken presented the team a wonderful framed memento of our visits to Iceland. That was it; the paperwork, the finances, heartache, logistics, food, sleepless nights and 16 hour days were over. As far as the RAF was concerned our conquest to reach Antarctica was complete. The only outstanding work I had to complete before departure was radio and newspaper interviews, which I had generated myself. I used the interviews to thank all our sponsors and to publicise our website, following which we received dozens of hits wishing us well.

What happens next, as with every expedition is the very heart wrenching experience of saying goodbye. While my heart and thoughts were firmly fixed on getting on the ice, your family and friends are experiencing a multitude of emotions, both happy and sad. During the first 2 weeks of October, Clare and I drove to see my mum, my 2 brothers and their families. Although I had experienced farewells before, this time, everything felt so much more serious, as the reality was, I may not come back. Portraying a positive outlook had become second nature which really helped me but as I said goodbye to each person, I gave them an extra tight hug and never looked back.

In addition for me, was the impending birth of our child. As we sat at home in the middle of October, Clare calming came down stairs, highlighting that she felt that her waters had broken and that we should take the journey to the hospital. As we had arranged for my eldest son Kieran to be down over this time, we dropped him off at Clare's mum and dad's while we went to the maternity ward. All I can say is, Clare was an absolute rock, as she went through a harrowing 54 hours, yes that was 54 hours of labour to finally give birth to our beautiful son Joshua. With Clare having spent so long in labour, Kieran had unfortunately missed seeing his brother, so Dean Singleton kindly drove him back to the airport for his flight back to Inverness. Before departing for the airport, I was a complete bag of nails as I said goodbye to Kieran. On one hand I was saying goodbye to one son, while my heart was being ripped apart by watching Clare go through so much pain as she gave birth to Joshua. Before departure, I had one final secret mission to complete and that was to ask John, Clare's father for her hand in marriage. My plan was to ask her to marry me, when I reached the South Pole. Thankfully, I received John's full blessing but trying to get him to congratulate me quietly was virtually impossible as I had asked him in his back garden and being partly deaf, he couldn't speak quietly. The final 24 hours before leaving was so difficult. I had tried to spend every minute of the last 2 weeks with Clare and Joshua, trying to fill the gap that I was about to selfishly create, but now we were stood at the airport holding each other. Clare and I had swapped presents months before hand; mine were in the boxes that we had packed back in September, but just before we separated, she handed me a picture of the 3 of us just seconds after Joshua had been born, which tipped me over the edge and into full blown tears. With both of us in floods of tears, we dried our eyes, gave each other another huge hug with Joshua between us and I left for the security gates. I couldn't look back as the guilt of what I was doing was too great. I hope and pray that after all the sacrifices I've made over the past 2½ years and especially the last hour of my life, this expedition is worth it.

Chapter 8
Exercise Southern Reach
RAF Antarctica Expedition, 1 November 2006 - 7 January 2007

Yes you've guessed it, this part of the book is a redacted version of the official post expedition report from our final objective to ski unsupported to the Geographic South Pole.

The aim, objectives, support and finances and various aspects will be covered within the diary of events. Any aspect that is not covered will be included after the diary as they contain answers as to what happened during this expedition.

Nominal Roll
The following personnel participated in Exercise Southern Reach:

* WO A Sylvester, *Headquarters Strike Command, High Wycombe*
* Cpl I Kirk, *RAF Kinloss*
* Cpl P Mainprize, *RAF Halton*
* Pita, *RAF*

The diary below gives a detailed account of the events that took place during Exercise Sothern Reach.

Wednesday 1 Nov 06
As I met up with Phil at the airport booking in desk, he was standing proudly in his dayglow coloured team jacket with his beaming smiley face. The process of being stopped by Customs with the teams ruggedised Pelican communications boxes was a pain as I had beacons, satellite phones, chargers all in the box. After a lengthy chat as to what we were doing, the gentlemen let us pass without any further hassle. I met up with Phil at the gate and settled down for a 9 hour

flight to Miami. Phil was sat just behind me and with our own entertainment system; I introduced him to watching the Catherine Tate Show. This incredibly funny comedian, actress and writer's show had Phil in hysterics. Anyone who knows Phil will know that Phil's laugh is extremely loud and addictive. Within minutes he had recruited the majority of the passengers around us to also switch on to this very funny show, with everyone giggling to themselves. It certainly brightened up this long and laborious flight. While in Miami we treated ourselves to a porky Burger King, followed by taking photos of proof of our short stay. Our next flight took us to Santiago, out of the 8 hr flight; I slept for 6½ hours, leaving me feeling a lot better. With only 90 minutes between landing and the take off to our last flight to Punta Arenas, we made it with just a few minutes to spare. What was interesting was the varying temperatures, in the UK 7 degrees centigrade, Miami 30 degrees, Santiago 12 degrees and Punta Arenas 2 degrees, this was to shape the things to come. After realising Phil's baggage had not arrived (it came on the next flight) we were met by Carlos from the Chilean Air Force (CAF). With immediate effect the CAF hospitality was second to none. The base lies only 1 mile from the airport, so we arrived on Station for an immediate audience with their Station Commander. A very warm welcome was provided after which we were being taken to our 2 man en suite rooms. This was a perfect start to conquest. With Kirky and Phil's bags arriving at 1530 hours, we headed back to the airport to liaise with Antarctica Logistics & Expeditions ALE personnel to retrieve our equipment as they had collected it in our absence. Within 2 hours we had received all our boxes, which had been packed up 6 weeks earlier at RAF Halton. Now back at the CAF base we were guided to their mess called "The Casino" for food and light refreshments. Having travelled for 37 hours we wrongfully thought we would have a quiet night in before Pita's arrival at 2330 hours. However, the CAF officers and troops had made other plans for us and proceeded to host us to a wonderful night's entertainment. As Pita was not due to arrive in Punta Arenas until later that evening, I stayed dry and off the beer. Once Pita was safely brought back to base we all settled down for a great nights rest.

Friday 3 Nov 06

Arose at 0730 hours, showered and took breakfast. At 0830 hours we were picked up by the CAF and taken to one of their hangers, which we used to unpack our boxes. After confirming everything had arrived safely and undamaged we prioritised our jobs by sorting and unpacking our food for 50 days. Using the accommodation block which was a lot warmer, we individually bagged up breakfasts, chocolate, drinks, peanuts and evening meals.

Breakfast consisted of 100 grams of porridge or 150 grams of muesli, supplemented with sugar, salt, chocolate, raisins, digestives biscuits and powered milk. This equals to approximately 650 /700 calories.

Peanuts are mega, providing an astonishing 2000 calories per quantity. Drinks generally gave us a further 500 calories, while Complan provided around 500 calories.

Our main meals were supplemented with an onion, garlic, ham or chilli Pemmikan, providing us a further 2000 calories. Each day's food weighed around 1.2 kgs to 1.4 kgs and was packed into batches of 1 week's worth to prevent any contamination from fuel or leakage. The team took around 11 hours to pack and weigh their food, as this aspect was so critical to our success; it has been an excellent day's effort. Phil's work with the rations back in the UK has proved to be awesome, his calculations were spot on.

Saturday 4 Nov 06

After an off the cuff social with the CAF until 2 am, I arose with a wee headache, so I walked down to the airport to hire a car. With a meeting arranged with Sean Chappel and his Royal Marines team and a Chilean Army Officer who had completed the crossing to the Pole in 1996, we set off into the city with David our CAF host. We received a very interesting lecture followed by lunch at the Chilean Marines base. It was a very momentous occasion, as Sean and I were leading the first ever British military expeditions to Antarctica, as we raised our glasses of Chilean red wine, we all wished for everyone's safe return. As we were in town we met up with Mike Sharp of ALE to discuss the plan for weighing and loading up our pulks onto the Illusion 76. Receiving warm complements on our planning greatly encouraged us, knowing we had planned our trip to the best of our abilities. After a wee social brew, we returned to base for a meal and postcard writing session. Today has passed quickly with so much happening. Although very excited, I am still feeling nervous and apprehensive about spending 7 weeks in one of the world's most hostile environments. I am very confident that we can do it; I guess it is the fear of the unknown that drives us to attempt these ventures in the first place.

Sunday 5 Nov 06

After another sociable evening with the CAF, we arose and sneaked a great breakfast in the Casino. Having access into the hanger was a real bonus as we concluded our equipment packing and put all our sponsors stickers onto our pulks, making them look just the part. After a quick lunch, we headed into town to purchase our fresh rations and assess the possibilities of buying a camcorder, the decision will depend on if we can recharge it via our solar panel. Returning to the base, we then concluded our food preparation, we are almost there with our packing! It's amazing just how much work is required, but it will definitely count when on the ice. The remainder of the day was utilised finalising our personal packing, comms box and devising various methods of attaching our compasses to our gortex jacket sleeves, as this will save many precious minutes while navigating south.

Monday 6 Nov 06

After an excellent night's sleep, we headed immediately for the hanger to put all our food into the pulks; we also split up the team kit to distribute the weight between the pulks. When Mark from ALE arrived to weigh our pulks, we were astonished to find the following:

Phil's weighed 100 kgs, Kirky and me 93 kgs and Pita 96 kgs. Somewhat a lot over the 85 kgs we had been expecting, so with a little swapping of the kit we all average out at 96 kgs, plus we have a further 15 kgs of fuel to pick up on the ice. I can see the months of pulling my tyres are going to come in handy. Kirky and Phil purchased the team camcorder, as it definitely charges via our solar panel. This news is awesome as this is a once in a lifetime experience, so to capture it on film for our friends and families is excellent.

Tuesday 7 Nov 06

I had a great night's sleep, followed by a bacon sandwich for breakfast. After which we headed up to the hanger to remove the Patriot Hill (PH) box (21 kgs of food and spares), which we have decided to bin and save a fortune in excess baggage fees. This was a box of equipment we were going to strategically leave behind at our landing location on the ice, should a disaster occur while on our voyage. As a team we calculated that adding 3 days' worth of food each in our pulks would compensate for any emergency rations. We also included a spare pulk harness and sleeping bag; these will be left at Patriot, purely as a comfort zone back up. Next we headed into the city for our safety brief from ALE and to meet our fellow explorers. The other teams consisted of:

- Sean Chappell + 3 Royal Marines:
  Unsupported to SP then kite ski back to PH

- 2 x 61 year old Americans:
  Supported to SP then kite ski back to PH

- Hannah McKeand:
  Unsupported to SP, attempting world record attempt 40 days

- Jamie and Kev, New Zealand.
  Unsupported to SP then kite ski back to PH.

There was also one lady who was purely flying onto Antarctica to photograph penguins!

An excellent brief was received explaining that temperatures had been extremely low in comparison to recent seasons due to high winds, resulting with potential expected temperatures of -50 degrees. I'm so pleased Phil was so insistent that we invested so much money purchasing the best equipment for these conditions. Unfortunately the brief also delivered the news that we are going to be delayed by at least another 2 days. The Twin Otters (light passenger aircraft adapted to land on ice) hadn't got into Patriot Hills until yesterday and the blue ice runway has had a lot of built up snow on it, which needs to be cleared. Additionally the cross winds were too strong for landing and taking off. We're all disappointed but this is Antarctica, one of the world's most hostile environments. On conclusion of the brief we completed a very traditional part of any explorer heading on to Antarctica, as we visited the Magellan statue in the centre of Punta Arenas. Magellan is the chap who invented the Global Positioning System, used by virtually everyone in the modern world. The theory is that by kissing the toe of the statue, this in turn will provide the team luck and a healthy return. It was only on our way home that our hosts explained that it is also a tradition of the local drunken youths to wee all over the toe, ho hum.

After lunch we provided a presentation to the CAF on how we had reached our position to date, we broke the lecture up into comms, rations, equipment and our route. Our hosts were very enthusiastic about our trip and we plan to provide another chat on our return. Having a spare 2 hours, I enjoyed a wee session in the gym, sweating out for the first time in a week. We're still having problems sending photo's to the website but Chris Toms is doing a sterling job collating our messages, cutting and pasting them, then sending them all in 1 message to our PDA. What a fantastic morale boost, I just wish we could send photos back. We've extended our time with the hire car, providing us more flexibility for the next 2 days.

Wednesday 8 Nov 06

We've definitely been delayed 2 days; the guys at Patriot are struggling clearing the runway and are still experiencing very high winds, which is very disappointing. First task this morning was to meet the new CAF Commanding Officer, a General who was a lovely character and was also very impressed with our plans, approach and intentions. This was followed by a stroke of genius by Kirky; he's managed to compress a photo small enough and has successfully sent it. *"Yeeehhhhhhaaaa he's only gone a bloody done it!"* Meeting up with David and Carlos we headed south to a wooden fortress, surrounded with heaps ancient Chile history. This location provided some magnificent scenery and was extremely kind of our hosts to organise. After taking a wee snack we headed back along the coast back into the city, where we took lunch in the officers' mess. Carlos allowed us to use his Internet so we could check emails and our website, the photos look great. After buying 50 stamps we returned to base, to write dozens of cards to the all the incredible people who have helped us reach this point so far. In the evening we met up with the Kiwi's, Sean's team and Hannah for a meal in the city. We had an excellent night swapping stories, with everyone holding back their frustration from our forced delay. Maybe tomorrow will bring better news with reference to the runway and high winds.

Thursday 9 Nov 06

The news is still bad; the guys are still trying to clear the sastrugi (a build up of parallel wave-like ridges caused by winds on the surface of hard snow) on the runway. So we headed into town to withdraw some money, post the cards and buy some salami, oh and we filled ourselves stupid on a McDonalds, yes even the most Southern city in the world has been invaded. Back at the base I paid our fees for food and accommodation, incredibly it only cost us £120 for all of us for 9 nights. Considering this was approximately the same amount paid in Iceland for 10 burgers and chips. Our Chilean colleagues have not only hosted us so well, they have saved the expedition a fortune in admin costs. The afternoon was spent searching for penguins but sadly to no avail, we did however see Emu's and Lama's. The amazing scenery of the prairie lands with the Patagonia Mountains in the distance certainly made up for the lack of penguins. After another lovely meal in the Casino, we picked up the days messages, once again filling our morale tank back to full. Using the car, we drove back to the main shopping area where we had eye balled a phone kiosk. We all took it turns to phone our love ones at home, ensuring them we were all ok and it was the weather that was stopping us from getting on the ice. Today has been a relaxing but this extension of living in a comfortable zone is going to make the transition onto the ice all that bit harder. I'm sure once on the ice we will soon pick up the routine and crack on with the expedition we have all dreamt of for so long.

Friday 10 Nov 06

After another great night's sleep, we headed into town to pick more money, post cards and pay ALE our excess baggage invoice and confirm any last minute admin queries. With all agencies informed including the MCC at RAF Kinloss and Kev Eaton, I sneaked a quick call to Clare who with Joshua and her parents had driven to Nairn to introduce the wee man to his brother Kieran. This was yet another sacrifice I had had to make witnessing my son's meet for the first time. Following the call we returned for lunch and returned the car. We've been on 3 hours standby all day so I sneaked in a quick cross training session in the gym, had 1 last long shower and a wee sleep as a decision should be made at 1800 hours. With update calls made every 15 minutes, the weather has improved, the runway is clear; all we need is the clearance from the crew. With minutes to go before I make the call I'm experiencing a roller coaster of thoughts and emotions about my fears and concerns. I'm sure once we're on the ice they will melt away and then we can get on with our task in hand. Again we received bad news, our flight was cancelled as the winds had picked up and the crew had postponed our start. We now wait for a call from the Patriot Hills at 0030 hours, eventually I fell asleep listening to my MP3.

Saturday 11 Nov 06

Fantastic, we were woken by David at 0540 hours, the winds have dropped and we are to be at the airport for 0800 hours. With a final pack and shower we donned our Antarctic clothing and headed off to the airport. We met up with the Marines and our fellow passengers and left only our bags on the bus. This saves heaps of time on security, as with no luggage we drifted through customs very efficiently. As this was Armistice Day, we all stood outside for a 2 minute silence, remembering and respecting our colleagues that had died or suffered during times of conflict. I've personally been in many locations during the 1100 hours ceremony but never as quite as important as today, because we were taking the military into another chapter of its history. With only the passengers of our flight to be cleared by security, we were ushered through customs and then to our bus, to rejoin our bags. It was now for the first time in the whole of the planning that I had actually seen the Illusion 76. How the hell was this humungous 4 engine Russian aircraft going to land on ice? I should also probably now admit that after attending over 30 aircraft crashes in my time with the RAF MRS, I am petrified of flying. So while standing having my photo taken in front of this eclipse of an aircraft, I was almost fossilised to the runway. The other issue was, I'd served in the RAF for over 23 years and been taught and brain washed never to trust or go near the Russians! So now, I was flying in a Russian aircraft, serviced by Russian technicians and flown by Russian aircrew and they were going to plant this flying tank on a blue ice runway. Trying to hide my fear, we boarded this huge aircraft and took our seats down the sides of the craft overlooking the freight of ALE and our pulks in the middle. Once sat, I realised this beast was similar to an RAF Hercules aircraft as there were no side windows neither. With a deafening roar we gently took off from Punta Arenas; the dream had started, our next stop would be the white desert of Antarctica. I'm writing this on the Illusion, I'm surprisingly relaxed but know that we could not have prepared for this any expedition any better, with the knowledge that we had. The in flight catering was very basic and amusing. The ALE staff stood up, erected a camping table in the middle of the aircraft and then proceeded to make sandwiches complemented with packets of crisps and chocolate bars, then strategically threw them around the cabin at the receiving seal like explorers.

After 5 ½ hours of flying we were given the heads up that we were 30 mins from landing at Patriot Hills. Watching the other passenger's anxious faces helped me to feel a wee bit better, as I wasn't the only person apprehensive about the landing. The pre flight brief had emphasised that we had to prepare for at least -20 degrees so we all donned on our various layers of clothing. The final seconds before touch down seemed to take an age but the first realisation that we had actually touched the ice was when we heard an horrendous roar of reverse engine thrust as we hit the 2 ½ mile blue ice runway. Having no windows didn't help as you could actually feel the aircraft gently sliding and twisting one way then the other while screaming along the ice at whatever speed. After approximately a minute we were still. My stomach eased an amazing relief as the aircraft turned around and headed back to its drop off point. The next event would be to stand on Antarctica. The cargo doors opened and a blinding mass of white appeared, the temperature was – 23 degrees with slight winds making the backs of our throats dry. Stepping down the ladder, then stepping onto the ice was overwhelming; we had made it, the first RAF expedition to set foot on Antarctica. With the Patriot Hills as an awesome backdrop, the view to the North was an immense expanse of ice with just minor shadows covering the surface, it looked breath taking.

After a few photos, we collected our 16 gallons of Coleman white fuel and moved onto the allocated camping area to erect our tents. With the other expeditions all having their own itinerary, we said our farewells and best wishes to the Kiwi's, Americans and the Marines, I did wonder when or if I would see them again. After digging up some fresh snow, we boiled up water for our evening meal, following which we met up with ALE's Patriot Hills coordinator "Di" a lassie from Grantown on Spey. After having all our kit, route, food and general admin scrutinised by Di and receiving warm admiration for our efforts, we settled in to our first night's sleep on the ice. We also moved our clocks onto Zulu time, so all despatches to our website and phone calls home would be at a more respectable time. The evening was very noisy, as the ALE staff were establishing their base camp, using snowmobiles and groomers to move the kit to its appropriate position. Di and her team would now stay here for the whole season to support the 100's of people who will be brought to Antarctica via the Illusion over the next 2½ months.

Sunday 12 Nov 06

I had a poor night's sleep, even though I wore my eye patches and ear plugs, as it is permanently 24/7 bright light and a constant wind blowing the tent. I think the reality of actually being on Antarctica was bubbling away inside me; hey we've only got 600 nautical miles to go. In the middle of the night, I opened my first card and present from Clare containing a wee chocolate and a book on Dads from Kieran and Joshua. She's so thoughtful, I just hope that she is enjoying my wee surprises as much back in the UK. The weather was – 22 degrees with a 10 kt wind, wow this was some wake up call when you first step out of your tent. With a good breakfast and with our kit on, we struck camp, packed our pulks and set forth south; the moment had finally arrived to get going. After 2 ½ years of planning and total commitment, this was it, we were off. No sooner did we get moving we started to traverse the blue ice runway, making our progress very slow as we were pulling 115 kgs.

Even having new skins to give us extra grip under our skis, gave all of us the skiing capability of Bambi. As we cautiously navigated around the edge of the Patriot Hills, escaping the crevasses, the wind picked up, greatly lowering the temperature, but the surface conditions greatly improved. With the occasional stop for juice and chocolate we continued until we realised Pita had a problem as he was already lagging behind. After disconnecting our traces (ropes) to our pulks, we skied back to Pita who was clearly struggling. We immediately put the Zarski emergency shelter up to find Pita was only wearing a next to skin top and his outer jacket. I was in disbelief. As Pita was suffering the first signs of hypothermia, we helped him take his outer gortex jacket off and put his spare warm clothing on which was in his pulk. What the hell was his thinking when we set off? Once warm, we set off again to complete our daily mileage of 8 miles. We stopped at 1600 hours and immediately got the tents up in 20 kt winds, the team did well, putting all the practices we had previously done in the CAF hanger into action. Inside the tent, I brewed up and then spent 90 mins adjusting the MSR cookers to accommodate these exceptionally cold temperatures. Then came the bad news, as at no time when we assisted Pita did he mention he was only wearing his gortex salopettes, he wasn't even wearing his long johns. As Pita removed his clothing I saw him wince with pain. In total horror I looked at his thighs that had various blisters and horrendous bruising as the blood vessels had exploded under his skin. He had sustained frostbite within only 3 hours of setting off. Words cannot express how I felt, as showing my frustration was just a waste of calories. I continued with boiling the water for the team, made up my food supplemented with pemmikan and then spent 30 mins in silence weighing up our options before breaking the news to Kirky and Phil in the other tent. Having thoroughly assessed his legs, I recognised by covering them with dressings and taking antibiotics, he could continue. For Christ's sake this was our first day! Phil and Kirky's comments were not printable, although they questioned the feasibility of returning him back to PH, we voted to keep him with us. Returning to my tent, I brewed up again, to fill our flasks for the morning's breakfast and to fill our Nalgene water bottles so we can hydrate throughout the night. I've had tingly sensations in my fingers and thumbs all day; I think it's a case of acclimatising to these extreme temperatures. It was reassuring to know that we all had the same experience. I always knew Antarctica was cold but this is very serious, Pita had made one mistake and was already making us pay.

Quote from Kirky's diary *"Antarctica is a truly awesome place. Since stepping off the plane and feeling your nasal and facial hairs freeze, you know it's cold!"*

Monday 13 Nov 06

Pita's blisters had congealed so we dressed them for the days skiing. After a quick breakfast but another long ice melting water boiling session, we struck camp and set off in – 18 degrees with a 10 kt winds, making it around – 26 degrees. We all immediately noticed Pita was slow but he still continued on for 2 legs covering an average of 2 miles. Putting the Zarski shelter up again, we rang Dr John based at Patriot Hills to ensure that we had given him the correct treatment and to advise him that we were stopping for the day. John had no major problems, he said thigh frostbite was common "ish" but if he didn't respond to the antibiotics, it would be endex for him. While putting up the tent, Kirky snapped a pole, so after putting the other tent up, I repaired it and then put their tent up with them. Crikey, I hope this is the end of the bad news; we've worked so bloody hard to reach this point. Well it's now 1735 hours and I've just celebrated by having my first Antarctic poo. Going to the toilet really has to be a very disciplined event. After crouching behind a snow wall to protect my bum from the wind, I would perform my business and by wearing a thin pair of gloves, I'd then put on my rubber marigolds to wipe my bottom with an icy wedge layer of snow. I can honestly say the wedge brings tears to your eyes, although it's a great relief to go the icy snow against my skin is very unpleasant to say the least. Having the snow wall was essential as the thought of having a 20 kt wind blowing up my chuff was bad enough, never mind wiping myself with ice. The reason why we use the snow is that the FCO had stipulated that we can only leave 3 things behind, pee, poo and foot prints. Thankfully I had won the argument about carrying our poo back to our starting point, but on no account was toilet paper allowed as this would litter Antarctica. Once I'd completed my business, I rubbed my gloves together removing any excess poo, then I collected another wedge of snow and cleaned my nether region, as hygiene is so important, regardless of the pain, I do feel that I'm starting to acclimatise to the freezing conditions, but I must keep my guard up as one mistake could really set me back.

Tuesday 14 Nov 06

I'm now writing my diary without my gloves on, maybe I'm starting to acclimatise to the temperatures. I had another poor night's sleep, the winds were gusting 30 kts, making it very noisy, and this with the permanent light is taking some getting used to. After replacing the dressings on Pita's legs, which have blisters still forming, we got away at 0930 hours. The conditions were perfect, light winds, great sunshine and the superb snow conditions. Making good progress, we came across an ascent of around 500 ft, which was very hard. Memories came flooding back of pulling tyres and knowing that all the effort had been worth it. Not only was it an ascent but also with the small sastrugi ridges it was a great effort. Thankfully we did it and once at the top we reached our first plateau. Here we made great progress, until we realised Pita was knackered so we called it a day at 7 ½ miles. Then picking up the same routine we put the tents up, dug the toilet shelter and unpacked our pulks for a comfortable night's sleep. As it had been warmer today around – 12 degrees, we noticed we had sweated, resulting with ice forming on the "inside" of our gortex jackets. Within the warmth of our tent, around +12 degrees, the sun radiates through, drying our clothes and warming our bodies, which is a lovely feeling. My mind played games with me as I had some funny thoughts today; I thought I'd heard a fast jet and then saw crampon marks in the ice ahead of us. Today has been the best so far, it's still very early days but I can handle a lot more of what we had done over the past 14 hours. Pita is still sore and slow but after a good chat with him tonight, he knows we're carrying his fuel and tent to lighten his load, he has to put the mileage over the next 3 days or we will reassess the options. We can do this as long as we keep our admin tight and have luck and good weather on our side, oh and good health with no more injuries!! It's now 2045 hours; I've just booked in with our daily call to our co-ordinators at Patriot Hills. This call is essential as we pass our location, health of troops, intentions, weather and any other relative information. As part of their remit, if we fail to check in after 2 or 3 days, an emergency evacuation could be established. Tonight's call is good, all is well and I'm off to read my book Angels and Demons, written by Dan Brown.

Wednesday 15 Nov 06

Once again I didn't sleep too well; I kept waking up either too hot or too cold. At 0700 hours I carried out the worst ritual of the day, getting out of my sleeping bag, with snow drops of condensation frozen to the inside of the tent. They quickly fall off onto your warm skin, encouraging you to get dressed as quick as you can. With 4 layers on and a down jacket, the 10 minutes of hell soon fades away. Then its breakfast, using the hot water out of our flasks made up the previous night, I mix my muesli with sugar, raisins and dried milk. This with a strawberry Complan makes a nice start to the day, although deep down I detest muesli. It's also very reassuring absorbing so many calories in me before taking on the challenges of the day ahead. Then its toilet time, using a snow wedge to clean my behind, once again putting my whole body into a freezing shock "Good morning Antarctica". It's a routine that we've learnt that if you eat the same volume of food at the same time every day, you will time your constitution at the same time each day. It's got to be achieved at some time, so the mornings work out best. Then finally we pack our pulks and take down the tents. Routine is not only very important, but it is essential for our survival as well. From waking till leaving takes around 2 hours 20 mins, most of this time is taken up by boiling the water required to keep us hydrated. All water bottles and flasks need boiling water in them, as even though the bottles are insulated the water would freeze. Today was yet another great day, the weather was great but slightly overcast, light if hardly any winds and temperatures around – 15 degrees, we actually covered our first 10 miles in 1 day, but I must admit I had a mare with navigating. All our compasses have bubbles in them, which is caused by the extreme temperatures they are operating in, remember they are strapped to the outside of our jackets and are permanently hit by the elements. I got frustrated with myself but soon got to grips with my negative thoughts.

Although I miss everyone heaps, I'm not yet missing my home comforts, life in a tent is as good as you make it, food is tasty and knowing I am actually on Antarctica is simply a dream. We've almost left the mountains today so maybe by tomorrow we will be surrounded by 360 degrees of white abyss, something I have thought about so many times. Erecting camp was an easy affair today with no wind, so both tents went up in minutes. With Pita, who is also feeling better, on cook duties I filled up a plastic bin bag of snow and ice so he can melt it for our water. It was also my turn to create a windbreak for our toilet area; well I reckon Barratt homes wouldn't have been too impressed with my brickwork but it achieved its aim. When I returned to the warmth of the tent, Pita had the cookers on melting the ice and as it had been 2 weeks since seeing Clare, it was time to open an envelope and a present from her. With more heart warming words in her card, I received more chocolate and an England Football Club quotations book. These little moments are huge in my heart.

Away from the physical and mental endurance we are experiencing every day, the psychological effects of an envelope and chocolate bar is immense. After my escape from reality, I plotted the Global Positioning System position for our daily situation report for Patriot Hills. Apart from my navigating mistake, today had been great. I hope the weather stays the same and we can get lots more mileage under our belts.

Thursday 16 Nov 06
Not a bad night's sleep, I still hate the first 10 mins of every day, extracting myself out of my warm cosy sleeping bag. Today I wore 2 pairs of socks, my gortex socks, big inner boot then the main boot, long johns and thermal salopettes, string vest, wind jacket, then my duvet jacket until I move outside,

when I swap it for my gortex jacket. I wear 3 pairs of gloves; a hat, neoprene mask and my fur hood permanently up. Once dressed, the cooker goes on and we settle down to boiling the water for today's adventure. The weather this morning is poor, strong winds and biting temperatures of –23 degrees, an approximate wind chill factor of around – 40 degrees, with only 40 metres of visibility. Once the tents were down we headed off with the gusting winds battering against our every move. Today was a far better navigating day for me. I've moved my compass from the arm of my jacket onto my outer mitt, so I can see our bearing almost all the time. The bubbles in the compasses are a real pain, especially in white out; it's ironic when the compass warms up in our tent at night, the bubbles disappear. Today was bloody hard, while we are out in the elements of Antarctica, we get constantly battered by the howling gales and are very conscious of the freezing temperatures that can bite you at a moment's notice, it's only when we are in the sanctuary of our tents can we relax. While being battered by the wind and in the relative safety of my hooded jacket, I find my thoughts drift all over the place. Today's thoughts were about cancer. Having lost my father to bowel cancer when I was only 18 years old, my mother suffering from breast cancer and my brother Ian having suffered skin cancer; these thoughts actually strengthened my efforts. Out here I was voluntarily fighting my battle, in comparison to the great discomfort and physiological hell they all must have gone through. The 8 hour day concluded by covering 8.04 miles, which in the conditions was great progress. The tents went up quickly and once again I helped to build the toilet area, which everyone greatly benefits from when having the daily constitution. You can only imagine what a minus 40 degree wind has on your bum n bits. Today's been another good day but fairly hard again, my fingers and thumbs are getting acclimatised but I now have a small ache in my left ankle as my skis tend to fall to the left. Also while putting up the tents, the pole accidentally belted me in the eye, which after packing it with ice has gone down but it is still very swollen and sore. Currently I'm chilling in the tent, about to read my football quotations book given to me as one of my secret presents from Clare. It's only in the secure and relative calm inside the tent, can I actually relax as I'm concentrating so hard on navigating or keeping up with the team.

Quote from Kirky's diary *"The majority of the time I have my hat on, either a ski mask/balaclava and hood up living in my own little world."*

Friday 17 Nov 06

I really enjoyed the funny book and I fell asleep on top of my sleeping bag, as at last the sun was shining, radiating heat through the sides of the tent. Well it did at least until about 2330 hours when I woke up absolutely freezing. I had my first great night's sleep, then processed through the same procedure, breakfast, morning constitution, packing and then off for another day in paradise. We've still a few mountains in view in the distance but mostly now it's a white abyss plateau, which makes navigation a wee bit sporty as you move from one sastrugi shadow to another. A lot of time is spent battling against the wind, making sure your head is covered and then drifting off into your own little world of tranquillity. Every hour we stop to eat chocolate and drink hot juice and then crack on. I personally drink my juice then eat the chocolate as it leaves nuts, raisins and melted chocolate between my teeth, which I enjoy for at least the first 5 minutes of the next leg. Each break is around 4 – 5 minutes as any longer makes you very cold taking 15 minutes of the next lead to recover.

Today we also ascended approximate 200 ft, which on a surface of sastrugi was very testing. We achieved another 8 miles today in 8 hours, which considering the weight of our pulks including Pita's food and fuel was great progress. I've still a problem with my left ankle, so I've built a ledge on the outer edge of my ski boot using food wrappers, as this will hopefully stop it from going over so much. Also my left eye is giving me great discomfort, I've had Pita put some cream into it tonight to try relieving the sharp pain. As Kirky is cooking, well melting ice, Pita and I are chilling out, drying out our sweaty kit, once again using the sun's radiating heat. My final job of the day was to actually name my pulk. I've decided to christen her Carley Snews, which is an anagram of Clare Wyness my girlfriend. Also to help pull her, I've written Kieran and Joshua on the front tips of my skis. The theory is, during my wee moments of hell, I can ask the boys to dig deep and help me pull Carley through the next hard section. These little things help so much during the endless hours of pulling my belongings behind me.

Saturday 18 Nov 06

Afraid I had another bad night's sleep; my eye is really inflamed and hurting constantly so I've decided to put a patch over it. Regardless of this, the day must go on, starting with building a shoe instep in my left boot. While fixing it

I had a brain wave and utilised a slab of pemmikan, it fitted a treat and once I got moving, it moulded into to the shape I needed. After the standard breakfast etc, we set off in below average conditions giving us 60 ft visibility and only light winds. It stayed like it all day making navigating very difficult and tiring.

We walked 20 paces, check compass, 20 paces, check compass and so on and so. Phil has amazing discipline, while Kirky and Pita lose their concentration after a short time. I was ok for the first 3 legs then my eye became really uncomfortable. I spent the remainder of the day virtually blind and following the closest pulk to me, I could see no more than about 5 ft ahead. Incredibly we achieved 9 miles in 7 ½ hours, which was exceptionally good going by the team. On arrival at our ice campsite, the tents and toilet were erected and we were melting ice all within 25 minutes; our admin is now up to speed. I've received lots of messages on the guest book so far, which are being collated by Chris Toms back in the UK and then sent to our PDA via a satellite signal, modern day comms is great, when it works. We crossed our first degree line today at 81 degrees; hey we've only 540 Nautical miles (Nm) to go. The reason I emphasise Nm, is that Nm is based on the circumference of the earth, and is equal to one minute of latitude. It is slightly less than a statute (land measured) mile for example 1 nautical mile = 1.1508 statute miles). As our maps/charts are calculated in nautical miles we are using this for our navigation. So our 600 nautical miles is actually equivalent to 677 statute miles.

Sunday 19 Nov 06

The weather was brilliant all day. I had a reasonable night's sleep, my eye is still very sore but it's improving. Same routine in the morning, set off skiing in perfect conditions, this was Antarctica at her best. We've now spotted some amazing mountains to our West, but the remainder of the 340 degrees is now just beautiful ice. We covered 11.2 miles in 7½ hours, proving how good the conditions are. Once the tents were up, which now only take 4 minutes each, it's my tents turn to cook again for 2 days. The system of cooking for 2 days then 2 off is great as it's your duty once every 4 days. One of the best things about being duty cook is you get to drink as much water as you want, not that I'm dehydrated but out here it is the little things that keep you going. Tonight I also brought the team together for an open chat, everyone's physically and mentally well, the morale is high and it was great to have some quality time together, without the battering winds and freezing temperatures biting into your conversation. Pita has got into a good routine of sorting out his legs, which are now as stable as we can make them. I did remind Kirky and Phil that we had discussed before departure the feasibility of swapping tents to vary the conversations in the evening. The looks on their face before they explained in the interests of Pita's health and safety, it was safer for me to remain with him for the remainder of the trip. Thanks troops, I love you too. To perk me up, I remembered that I had an envelope from a mystery person to open. It was Clare's mum and dad, Ann and John, who wrote such positive and encouraging words, this was just what I needed as I'm tired and need some sleep, it's been 8 days of hard physical exertion and I need some rest.

Quote from Kirky's diary *"I chipped my tooth today on some rock hard frozen chocolate, not looking forward to seeing the dentist now."*

Monday 20 Nov 06

Another average night's sleep, as I'm on cook I don't want to sleep in and extend the day any further. I boiled water for all our flasks and meals and then we were off. Its overcast and a wee bit windy, making the temperature around -25 degrees, which we all seem to be getting accustomed to. Throughout the day during the legs, you have your hood up, your goggles on, you're masked up and then with your skis and poles hitting the ground, you hear some very strange noises. Today I actually thought I heard a cow, donkey and more fast jet aeroplanes, you know there's nothing there except ice and snow but this place does have a strange effect on you. I did think a remarkable thought today that with so few explorers ever attempting this journey we were the first people to ever step on the ground that we are currently covering. What a proud and amazing thought!!! On arrival of camp, we had covered 8 ½ miles in 5 ½ hours, this is great. Also Kirky wasn't firing on all 4 cylinders today so it made heaps of sense to stop while the going was good, to get some extra relaxation and chill out time. Also in 2 day's time we are extending the mileage to 12 miles per day, so the rest is good. I also seized the chance to talk to the BBC Look North and BBC 3 Counties with reference to future interviews. We also updated Kev Eaton, all's well at his end but he has asked us to contact him every 2 days, as he is being approached by lots of different agencies about our progress. Brian my brother has organised the BBC Look North chat and ironically all 4 of us originate from their broadcasting area. Brian has done more for the expedition than the Central Office of Information who are being paid to advertise our exploits! Today was harder, meaning I had to concentrate on my pace a lot more. The guys are all moving well and I averaged around 2.4 miles with my 90 minute lead, which was faster than yesterdays by .1 of a mile, but hey they all count. It's now while I'm laying here in the tent I get time to reflect about things at home, with all the fantastic messages being received on our PDA, we are all overwhelmed but tonight I received the majority of the messages. Knowing everyone is routing for us helps so much.

Tuesday 21 Nov 06

Decent night's sleep, but still sweating too much as my sleeping bag is damp every morning. On cook again while Pita sorts out his legs, so I'm first up getting the water boiled for our day's adventure. With tents down, we set off at 0925 hours; everyone is recouped and ready for our last day of 8 miles. We've now settled into a good pattern and pace. Pita goes first, then Phil, then me and finally Kirky. Phil is bagging almost 3 miles during his 90 mins leg, he's certainly the fittest out of the team, I just hope being slim, that he doesn't burn himself out so early in the trip, but he is like an ox. We have spoken about it and he's very happy and has thought about it already. While leading from the front everything is simply white snow and ice; you fix on your bearing of 135 magnetic variation degrees and aim for the next shadow of sastrugi. This is easier said than done, as no sooner you take your eye off it, your back to your compass to verify which direction it was again. The bubbles in compasses are still a big pain in the bum. This small price does not take away the awesome beauty of our surroundings. It's almost like walking/skiing on a lake of frozen milk. We still have peaks in the distance, which we first spotted 3 days ago; I think tomorrow they will be gone, leaving us at last with the 360 degree of white abyss. It appears my love for Antarctica is growing by the day; she is so vast, so beautiful, yet so perilous. I set the test beacon off today to verify our location; it does give you that little piece of security in this hostile and extremely wild environment.

I'm currently chilling listening to my MP3, reading Angels and Demons with Clare's picture by my side. Life is as good as it can get. We covered 10 miles in 6½ hours, but it was very cold again at -27 degrees. Tomorrow we start our set of 12 milers for the next 10 days. We've snags with one of the Satellite phones, we simply can't get a power supply to it and its battery is dead. I've informed the Patriot Hills, MCC, Kev Eaton as if our other phone breaks, we would then revert to a test beacon every night between 2045 – 2145 hours, I pray this doesn't happen, as we will also lose our 2 way with our website. Without telling the guys, I'm bloody furious as I had contacted the phone maker to ask for spares and was reliably informed, the phones are virtually unbreakable, you won't need them.

Wednesday 22 Nov 06

I had another bad night's sleep, as I'm trying to stop my bag from getting wet with my sweat. I also laid awake trying to resolve our comms issue, unfortunately though nothing came to mind. We them followed the same routine for breakfast and taking the tents down.

Today's weather was awesome; I never wore my outer gortex jacket all day, although I did get chilly during our 5 minute breaks. It stayed around – 10 degrees all day so maybe things are starting to warm up. I managed a 2.7 miler today during my lead, as I felt very strong and paced out all day, covering our first 12 mile day. We've also now only got 494 miles to go so that is yet another mile stone under our belts. With tents up, Kirky and I tried to fix the charging wires to the Iridium, but after 2 hours, there's still no power. I sneaked a 3 minute call to Clare as I knew that she would have driven from Scotland down to Faringdon. I told her of the analogy I had used today about comparing our 4 to 5 minute stops, with her stopping at service stations on her way down. I also broke the news that if we were unable to repair the other phone, this maybe our last call before returning to Chile. Although it tore me apart I had to tell her, as operational calls come first. I've noticed tonight that all my fingernails are growing except my thumbs, which are quite numb at the ends, but I'm not worried about them as yet. It's 2145 hours and I need sleep, that's now 11 days of physical exertion, averaging 7½ hours a day that could leave around 34 days to go, what a thought to go to sleep on.

Quote from Kirky's diary *"This morning the mountains in the distance looked like a volcano as there was little wisps of cloud coming off its summit."*

Thursday 23 Nov 06

Good night's sleep at last, I woke up to bright sunshine and 15 kt winds at around – 20 degrees. A good night's sleep actually equates to waking every 3 hours. With breakfast and the tents down I did a bit of filming of prepping for the day and then into the biting winds we set off. I've made a deal with the troops, that I would do all the filming while they take the still photos. This first leg found me a little sleepy but after 90 minutes and 2.5 miles covered I soon woke up. Nose bag, also known as our admin breaks are usually around 5 minutes as no sooner have you drank your juice and eaten your chocolate, you're so cold that you need to get going on the next leg. I took the third lead and covered 2.6 miles, I'm happy with that, as the sastrugi is getting a lot more frequent. With all 4 leads complete, we still had 2 miles to go, so I took another leg to finish off the day's mileage of 12 miles. Leads 5 and 6 of each day are completed on a voluntary basis, the guys are all happy to take their turn as they know their aiming towards a night's rest. I have noticed that Kirky and Phil are very keen to volunteer as they know they'll cover more distance. With the tents and toilet built, it was Pita's turn to cook, so it's a great excuse to dry out our damp and now smelly kit. I must admit I do smell a little, but not as bad as Pita's frostbitten legs, which smell horrible. I did start the day lethargically but tonight I'm back to firing on all cylinders again. We are only 1 mile away from the 82nd degree; that's a 1/5 of the way. Not counting any chickens, as this is bloody hard work all round, we just need luck, health and good weather on our side. Its 2145 hours, Pita's still cooking so I'm going to listen to my music and sink into my photos in my waterproof wallet.

Quote from Kirky's diary *"It's good having someone like Phil along because he is very disciplined in himself and pushes everyone hard."*

Friday 24 Nov 06

Well I had to swap ends of the tent last night; Pita's snoring even surpassed my ear defenders. I actually got in around 6 hours last night, although I feel I need more. 0700 hours came too quickly but got up; as I started Pita's cooking for him, while he tended to bandage his legs for another day of skiing ahead. Outside was 20 kts winds with a temp of around -40 degrees; wow someone has turned the temperature down in this giant freezer. We set off with lots of sastrugi in our way, which also has soft drifted snow around the sides, making the pulks sink deeper before breaking through to the good ice below. With Pita clearly struggling we only covered 4.4 miles in 3 hours. We took Pita's remaining fuel off him, making his pulk 12 kgs lighter. This made a great difference, with Kirky's lead ticking 2.5 miles, followed by mine of 2.6 miles. Phil then voluntarily took on the last lead to bring us up to the day's requirement of 12 miles. The temperatures today have been Baltic, even now while writing this at 2200 hours, with the sun blazing through the sides of the tent; it's not as warm as it has been over the past week. Today has been our hardest yet, even though we did 8 hours of physical work, it's starting to catch up with us, with exerting ourselves each day. I must admit the temperatures today have scared me a little. You can only wear 1 glove for less than 2 minutes or else your fingers explode with pain, there is no way I will be complacent, as Antarctica will make you pay if you let your guard down. It's time for sleep, we've another 12 miles tomorrow, and I hope the foundation of this distance is settling in as next it's 10 days of 15 milers.

Saturday 25 Nov 06

At last a good night's sleep, but Pita is stinking badly with his frostbitten legs. Did the normal routine, but noted Phil and Kirky's tent had a small tear, which will need repairing tonight. The first 2 legs went really well, considering the temperature is now down to around -50 degrees with a battering wind of 30 kts, making the surface very slippery even under our ski skins. The 3rd leg was an ascent from hell and lots of other explicatory words. Although it slowed our pace down, Kirky led it really well, as now we have swapped our leads around so I pick up no. 4, which I'm very glad of. Then taking over from Kirky, Carley Snews my pulk continued to topple over causing me great frustration. Every time I got into some pace the sastrugi would topple my pulk over. I've ensured all my heavy kit is at the bottom so I think it's down to the way I cross the ribs of ice. Venting your frustration costs calories, so I continued in my own hooded world, swearing at myself. With the conditions deteriorating further, the winds getting stronger, lowering the temperature even further, I only managed 2 miles; this was a bloody awful lead. The next 4 ½ hours we battled against the worse conditions so far, finally reaching our 12 mile point after 9 hours. After completing such an exhausting day, everyone got stuck into getting the tent up in the very strong winds, which allowed Phil to put his sewing skills into action by repairing the torn tent. The extra long porches on these Hilleberg tents are fantastic, giving you lots of space to complete your admin in. As we had worked for 9 hours on the ice then lost more time as Phil repaired the tent with desperately cold hands, we split the cookers tonight and completed our own cooking, to save time and to give some warmth to both tents. It's now 2200 hours, it's been the hardest day so far and that's 3 on the trot. I hope the winds subside, statistics show that Antarctica at this time of year has an average of 6 kt winds, yeah right, not from where I'm sitting. I am at my lowest point today, Antarctica has thrown some hefty punches at us today, but no way is it going to beat me or my team. I know today was tough, but I also know within myself I can take more, the scary thing is though, just how much more? For the first time during our time on the ice I headed straight into my sleeping bag, as it really is that cold tonight.

Sunday 26 Nov 06

Had an average night's sleep due to the battering winds, fortunately around 0430 hours it calmed down a little. Normal routine then we were off at 0925 hours with the surface of the ice being very hard, which the pulks are not enjoying at all. Also my lead had another ascent, which added to my frustration. I am learning, this is all about discipline regardless of the distance covered during a lead, it is still a few metres closer to our dream. I've taken to singing all sorts of songs out loud, from Phil Collins, Pink Floyd to Scottish folk. The great relief for the team is with the constant winds, they do not have to endure my dulcet tones. You all know that songs can take you back to a certain moment in time, incredibly today I hummed the instrumental theme to Local Hero by Mark Knophler. This was one of the last tracks that I had shared with my father, so as skied, I openly cried with my tears flowing, which were all hidden by my ski goggles. Once again though we completed our 12 miles thanks to Phil's last lead, which was amazing; he certainly is our guarantee to complete our day's mileage. With tents up by 1830 hours and in calmer conditions I seized the chance to speak to my family. Hearing Clare's, Kieran's and my mother's voice from such an isolated location is surreal. Their worlds were continuing as normal, while mine was being slowly torn apart by this beautiful yet hostile environment. Keeping the call as upbeat as possible, I'm sure neither of them picked up my anxieties. While chatting, I almost lead myself into a false sense of security, but as the calls ends, the silence instantly brings me back to reality of my challenge. Then my internal clock starts to tick as my roller coaster thoughts try to work out when I can chat to them again. It's now 2200 hours and I'm still buzzing from the phone calls, also the winds have almost dropped, I only hope the surface softens for the morning. I've got twinges in both my ankles so I've massaged some Volterol cream on them, to calm the swelling down. My eye is improving, the eye drops have worked and I've almost got clear vision in it again. It's very apparent, that nothing repairs itself quickly down here, if it repairs at all after looking at Pita's legs.

Monday 27 Nov 06

Another average night's sleep, as once again I'm concerned about sweating too much and soaking my sleeping bag, oh well at least I got 4 hours in. We did the same routine, then set off with virtually no wind and temperatures around -25 degrees. Today was spent mostly working through fields of sastrugi, which really is testing our patience and fitness. The good news is, now the temperatures have risen the surface is less slippy. I only managed 2 miles on my lead proving again how desperate the conditions are. I'm now having problems with my right ankle leaning over with virtually every step. So once again I've utilised another pemmikan and created another improvised insole. I'm currently on cook boiling up 12 litres of water, which is the quantity required every night. As you have to melt it from ice it takes nearly 2½ hours of constant melting to produce this boiling water, oh for the use of a kettle and 240 volts. Got to admit after my lead at 1600 hours, I announced that war between Antarctica and I had been declared, I know I won't beat her but if she would just allow me a wee break now and again from the pain, we could be friends. All I want is to reach the centre of her but I know we've still got 434 miles to go. Knowing everyone is supporting me helps me heaps but it can put lots of pressure on me to succeed, I can only try my best, which so far has gone well. You may wonder why I refer to Antarctica as her/she. I can only describe it from a man's perspective, Antarctica is a desert of limitless beauty and for that and the way she has a stubborn mind of her own, I refer to Antarctica as a female. I'm confident, that all female explorers will refer to Antarctica as him. While cooking I read my cards and books from Clare, Kieran and Joshua. I'm sure they understand just how hard this challenge really is. I must quote it's a lot harder than I could have ever trained for or imagined. Tomorrow's another 12 miles, we've now done 16 days of physical work without a break. I can see it starting to show on all of the team but the morale is still high. I delivered the hot water to Kirky and Phil, in return they gave me the PDA, to read our messages. Apart from reading the letters I brought with me, reading the messages on the PDA is the only trace of reality I feel I have with the real world away from this frozen abyss. Tonight I've learned that Joshua is now 10lbs 8 ozs, I wonder is Clare managing any sleep with feeding him that much.

Quote from Kirky's diary *"At one point, I took my skis off and even went onto hands and knees to pull my sledge clear of a snow bank. Al kept falling over which was hilarious, although he didn't think so."*

Tuesday 28 Nov 06

I went for it last night, as I desperately needed a night's sleep, so I closed my sleeping bag and sweated all night. I did sleep well but my bag as expected was wet this morning. I've worked out that so far I have only averaged 4½ of sleep per night. I'm duty cook so once again I was up early to get the cookers on for the troop's water. After a rather generous portion of porridge, which I still detest, I venture out for my morning constitution. Without going into too much detail, the effects of pemmikan is quite apparent, taking several minutes of bare arsed time to start any form of delivery. Thank goodness for the wind breaks. We got away around 0920 hours in clear skies, good surface with 20 kt winds, temperature was around -25 degrees. Felt heaps better today, the pemmikan in my boots is working a treat. As the surface is better, we're moving a lot quicker but also we still have to navigate around the fields of sastrugi, which is very frustrating but essential. I managed 2.57 miles on my lead today, which as no 4 in line is very good. With 7 days of 12 miles under our belts I was hoping my pulk will be a lot lighter as we approach the 15 milers, in 3 days' time. I know the rest of the guys are thinking that way as well. Tonight I boiled up lots more litres of water, but we also spoke to Harry Gresham from BBC Look North. It goes out tomorrow, so I left a message on Mums phone to give her the heads up. To be truthful I was that tired I wasn't that interested about the interview, but as my brother Brian had worked so hard to co-ordinate this and that it sells the RAF and spreads to the word about our exploits it's all part of our adventure. It's 2120 hours, I'm waiting for Phil to collect their flasks and also drop off the PDA so I can read any messages. Once again there were lots of great posts all wishing us well and congratulating us on our progress so far. I spent the rest of the evening planning a trip to Crete for my mum in

May of next year. Clare's great friend Jackie and her parents Margaret and Jack are such wonderful characters, I know mum would love every element of this holiday. Again these thoughts give me a break from the permanent anxious thoughts I have throughout the day. I feel Antarctica doesn't allow me to relax.

Wednesday 29 Nov 06

Great night sleep at last even had a dream about being in a prison. Awoke to get the cookers on and prep the flasks for the guys. Tents down and we were off, clear skies, light winds and a great surface yehhaaa! This was the best and quickest days skiing yet. We covered the 12 miles in 7 ½ hours including my lead of 2.7 miles up hill. With the conditions being good, I found myself concentrating hard on keeping up the pace as the guys really moved well today. It's good though as we know we're starting our 15 milers in 2 days. Back in the tent, it's the end of week 4 and I've opened another letter and a book on Smashing Dads from Kieran and Joshua. Realising we had full power and 2500 minutes left on the phone, I had a 14 minute call to Clare. She's had her 6 weeks post natal check and all is OK. This was our first call without tears, I have a completely different life to return to but for now, I've still a few hundred miles to ski. My morale is 110%.

Thursday 30 Nov 06

Reasonable nights sleep, the sun radiated through the tent till around 0100 hr, then I got into my bag and dreamt about jungles and monkeys. During our normal routine I'm now forcing myself to drink 2 Complan drinks as well as my porridge etc. I'm starting to feel thinner and I can tell, as now when leaning forward to tie my boots, there is no longer a belly restricting my movement. With drinking and eating more I'm fighting to keep the weight on, although I know I will lose weight; I just wonder, how much? As we started today the weather was very bleak, about – 40 degrees, with very poor contrast, making it very difficult to make out the ground in front of you. Fortunately after the first leg, the sun started to burn through, improving both the visibility and pace. I reached 2.9 miles with my lead today, which is my best distance yet, I felt my pulk is starting to get a wee bit lighter, probably around 85 kgs, which was the weight we tried to aim at as a starting weight. My skiing is improving as the pulk gets lighter, but the hills are still bloody hard work. We did our 12 miles in 7.5 hours, which is fine as we only have 1 more day before the 15's start.

Another great thing today, we've crossed the 83 degree line, so only 7 degrees to go. Hey they all count. I had comedians come into my thoughts today, Stan Boardman, Harry Enfield, Steve Coogan, Little Britain and Catherine Tate, I have no idea why, it is very strange how spontaneous thoughts come into your head in this open mass abyss of ice. I phoned my brother Brian, his wife Jane and their children Jodee and Daniel thanking them for all their messages of encouragement but also for arranging the BBC Look North interview, all of the guys really appreciate what Brian is doing for us. Well its 2140 hours, it's early so I'm going to read my book and get some sleep.

Quote from Kirky's diary "It's hard to explain really, but this place is so magical and awe inspiring, it really does take your breath away, who would have thought 2½ years ago, I would be here?"

Friday 01 Dec 06

Not so good night's sleep, Pita's legs stink, every time he moves I get a waft of dead tissue, which is bloody awful, but I know he's taking the antibiotics and therefore keeping any further bacteria at bay. 0700 hours comes around all too quickly, but it's another disciplined routine that we must stick to, which includes peeling yourself from your homely sleeping bag. Same routine of breakfast and tents down. Today was sunny with a 20 kt wind, the temperature was low again we reckon with the wind chill factor it was as low as -50 degrees, this does make a huge difference to your mental approach, as you know it is going to be bloody hard again, battling against the elements. We took a steady pace throughout the day; I only achieved 2.4 miles as my pulk was all over the place, while we crossed some treacherous sastrugi fields. Every time I get into any sort of decent pace, my pulk rolls over; it's all down to how I cross the line of sastrugi. It was at the end of my lead, I noticed everyone was knackered, so with a 3 to 1 decision, we stopped and concluded the day at 11.9 miles; also we stopped at a very good flat camping area, not contaminated with sastrugi. Additionally finishing at 1700 hours, knowing the 15 milers start tomorrow is also added bonus. Throughout the day I've been thinking about how I can truly explain just how physically and mentally hard this challenge has been. Over the years I've ran over 15 marathons, walked dozens of 30 mile plus mountain days etc, how can I explain about how it feels to cover 201 miles in 20 days, stretching out towards the South Pole, towing over 100 Kgs of kit without sounding like I'm exaggerating the experience? I will just tell them like it is. The last 2 hours of today was shear hell. I'm really feeling the physical aspects, even though I have trained so hard. The only experience I can compare each day is like hitting the transparent marathon wall. In both cases, regardless of how hard it hits you, you've still got to finish the race, then put your tent up and survive another night. Tonight I've eaten 2 meals, which although I'm famished it is very hard to digest such large portions as my stomach shrinks with exertion. Having planned to increase my meal intake, the plan is working well as I now need those extra calories, also we start the 15 milers tomorrow. The extra mileage is worrying me a little but we can only do what our bodies will allow us to do, but most importantly, we must pace it correctly. I concluded the day by opening up another surprise envelope. Today was from Emma & Lee Tucker and her lovely parents Syd and Debs. I worked with Emma while at Andover, she's the type of lassie that walks into the room and brightens up any dull situation. As soon as I opened the envelope, my whole world and mood lightened up again, I am so lucky having so many people support me.

Saturday 2 Dec 06

Last night, Phil and Kirky, came up with an excellent idea to improve the actual time that we are moving. They have noticed over a period of 10 days, that the weather and temperatures would be better if we push our movements by 90 minutes forward, which means as we will be moving later in the evenings, we stand a better chance of potentially better conditions. This is a great idea and I whole heartedly agreed with their suggestion. Ironically as we awoke today, the weather and contrast was terrible. For the first 6 hours, the visibility was down to approximately 1 metre and with a fresh layer of snow made the contrast between snow and sky virtually blind. On several occasions, without realising, I entered sastrugi fields and walls up to 3 feet tall either side of me, resulting with me having to take my skis off and pull my pulk out of huge holes. This is infuriating, each time destroying my morale a bit further. Then miraculously the visibility cleared, we once again had a horizon and we were back to full speed for the last 3 hours. Antarctica plays hard and constantly pulls on your emotional heart strings, you have to keep focused on the challenge, as if you let her creep into your mind, she will bite you with unspeakable pain. Incredibly we ticked 10.6 miles, which under the conditions is great mileage. As we lost 4.4 miles, we aim to do 16 miles tomorrow, obviously weather depending. Tonight,

I spoke to Clare again, it's almost like she absorbs my pain and concerns as no sooner the call finishes, it feels like my batteries are recharged and ready for the next round of this fight.

Sunday 3 Dec 06

Had a reasonable night's sleep, although I woke up sweating, which once again soaks my bag, but 5 hours kip is great. Pita's legs are still bad so I did his breakfast again, the consolation is being closer to the cookers makes it a warmer start. With all the flasks filled and tents down, we set off in great weather at around -20 degrees. I'm only wearing 3 layers today, which makes things more comfortable. Everyone put in some great leads today at speed, including me; as I ticked 2.9 miles including a wee incline. We finished off completing 16.1 miles in 9½ hours, our furthest distance yet. Although tired, it's a great feeling as we caught up the 1.1 mile lost yesterday and we know by the time we come to the 18 milers, our pulks will be approximately 18 kgs lighter, which is a great thought in our grey matters. Just been to see Kirky and Phil and received another heap of messages, which is awesome for morale. It's 2340 hours, although early I need the rest, today was very rewarding and I've got it all to do tomorrow and the next and the next, well weather depending.

Monday 4 Dec 06

Another 5 hours of sleep, I am quite tired now, considering we've been going for 23 days. I'm feeling very healthy apart from my heels, which maybe the starting of plantar facia. Same routine but I have noticed that I am losing a lot of weight, it's nothing to worry too much about, but my ribs are showing. We set off in decent weather but it soon deteriorated down to no visibility during my lead. I was raging with frustration as not only was I falling over but my pulk was tipping over virtually every couple of minutes, today Antarctica won the battle. I was so grateful to Kirky who took over the last 20 minutes of my lead as he claimed he had some visibility. I only found out afterwards, that Kirky couldn't see anything at all but through shear grit and determination he blasted through. We battled on for 9 hours and travelled 12 miles, which in the horrendous conditions was very respectable. Finishing at 2000 hours, we quickly put the tents up and dug out the toilet. With time on our side, we all utilised the phone, tonight I spoke to Kieran in Inverness. For a 9 year old, he had a very good grasp on what we were attempting and said his school were also monitoring our progress on our website. It is so heart warming speaking on the phone and helps you feel so much closer to your loved ones. It's now 24 days since we have seen anyone else apart from the 4 of us. This baron, hostile yet beautiful place is very lonely, carrying the pictures of my family gives me that little warm feeling that my love ones are not too far away. Clare's waterproof wallet is perfect for the job as it's tucked inside my next to skin top.

Today although very hard again has passed very quickly which is yet another day closer to our destiny. Tonight, I thoroughly enjoyed 2 x chicken curries, supplemented with a whole pemmikan followed by more hot drinks, visiting a restaurant will never seem the same again. It's now 2300 hours; it's the earliest finish yet since moving to the new time schedule, but I'm knackered.

Tuesday 5 Dec 06

Flipping heck, best night's sleep I've had so far. I obviously needed it, 7 hours is a record but I feel so much stronger now for today's adventure. I'm writing my diary in the morning, as I'm duty tent warmer/cook tonight. The ritual of getting up, having breakfast, avoiding the smell of Pita's legs, the delivery of empty flasks and the warming up of the other half full flasks, then my constitution is just becoming a normal way of life in Antarctica. Oh how life will change when we have electricity, toilets, kettles, showers oh and no flipping porridge. The ice sores on my chin are still very tender with the scabs getting increasingly bigger. It happens when the ice builds up on your beard, then creeps towards your skin then burns. The other minor things are, I still have numb thumbs and the skin on the edge of my fingers is flaky. E45 is helping but it is strange that my thumbnails are not growing. Also I've gained some sores on my thighs, I think they are from the prevailing winds. Kirky has the same, it's definitely not frostbite, but they're weird and sore. What we've all noticed is once you have sustained a cut or sore, it is extremely difficult to let it heal as we are constantly moving, Pita's legs are looking horrible but still cleanish. It's now 2340 hours and I'm still boiling water. We've had a great day covering 16.1 miles in 9½ hours. The weather stayed great all day and we even had a view of our first mountains for 2 weeks. It's the start of the Theil range which means we are almost ½ way. We've also moved our bearing to the right a wee bit, which is deliberate, as we have some known crevasses on the 80 degree line, which we need to circumnavigate around in about 5 or 6 day's time.

Wednesday 6 Dec 06

Another average night's sleep, every time I wake up, the stench of Pita's legs has the effect of smelling salts. As I'm cook, I boiled up and we set off in 15 kt winds and temperatures around -30 degrees, with clear skies. Today has been a mega roller coaster of emotions, basically from the first leg I was almost energy less, although I dug in deep, there was nothing. It was like the previous 24 days had caught up with me and hit me like a tonne of bricks. By leg 2, I was even drawn to tears with thoughts of what the hell was going to do, what on earth is this South Pole challenge all about? Both these thoughts were topped off with my amazing lead weight guilt having left Clare behind, bringing up our new born baby. When it came to my lead, I tried to vent my frustration by going off like a bat out of hell. Although, the speed didn't last too long as my lead soon came across another sastrugi field from hell and was also up hill. Thankfully my pulk didn't fall over too often but I've never been so thankful for the end of my 90 minutes. Legs 5 and 6 were somewhat of a blur as I was now running on empty for 3 hours. Trying to blag my way through it with the troops while putting the tents up was pointless, both Phil and Kirky commented on my condition, after 5 weeks together you can't hide anything. Now while reflecting on the day in the tent I think that although I've been slow all day, oh and as our 15 miles was mainly up hill, I should be ok tomorrow for another 15 or 16 miler. It's now 2330 hours and I feel Antarctica had dealt me another punch below the belt. Throughout the day I had felt so exposed and so insignificant in this white void of hell. At no stage did I feel scared but when you know there's still around 320 miles to go, you do wonder if your body and mind will let you complete this once in a life time challenge. I'm sure my determination will get me through as long as my body allows me, as I need closure from the last 2 ½ years of planning, then and only then can I transfer my energy into my family. I've even got a wee smile on my face as I'm about to head outside for a pee and it's around -25 degrees. I could use my pee bottle but heading outside will leave me with an impregnated vision of my beautiful surroundings that I will fall asleep with. That really was a day and a half.

Quote from Kirky's diary *"I had a very rough day. I felt weak and found it hard to maintain the pace. We still did 15 miles and it all seemed up hill. I hope I feel better tomorrow."*

Thursday 7 Dec 06

Only got about 4 hours of sleep, it was so hot with the sun radiating through the sides of the tent, also Pita's legs were stinking really bad. Did breakfast as normal and set off for around 1100 hours. During the first lead that Pita led, he appeared very slow but I put it down to his thighs hurting him. Unfortunately I was wrong, it was his Achilles tendons. We managed 2 legs worth of distance covering 4.8 miles and then put up a tent as he was in so much pain. I spoke to Ben the Patriot Hills medic as Dr John was up at Mt Vincent recovering 3 frostbitten casualties from the mountain. Basically Pita potentially has tendonitis; we rested for the remainder of the day, while he kept his ankles on ice. Also today Pita broke the news to me that we we're almost out of antibiotics. I questioned this as we all brought 10 days of prophylactic medicine with us, including antibiotics, pain killers etc. In a very quiet voice he advised me that he had not brought his allocation of medicine with him. I'm struggling now to express how I feel as in the back of my mind, I've always known we had 40 days of medicine. Once again I was bloody furious. Immediately, my mind went into overdrive, calculating how many days Pita would have to endure knowing his legs were deteriorating badly. The team had made a pact that we would have no external support as this expedition was totally unsupported. We did consider asking for a Twin Otter to literally throw a packet of antibiotics out of the aircraft window while on route to the South Pole while carrying tourists, but subsequently found out from ALE that this was not an option. Although I remained calm, I've given him the option, make 15 miles tomorrow and keep up with the team or he's getting picked up by a Medevac. I knew that this would contravene our intentions but I'm so annoyed with him. We now need to do 10 x 15 and 9 x 18 miles to reach the Pole on the 27th Dec, that means no bad weather or further hold ups, which we are fully capable of. We potentially have 1 day flex to get picked up from the South Pole on the 28th evening in order to make our flight back on the 29th afternoon. I feel this is getting tight but we must endeavour to aim for it. The next Illusion flight is on the 4th Jan 07, so fitness (health) depending, oh and also have weather and luck we hopefully won't have to take this flight but it is always an option. With time on our hands, we made some additional hot drinks, ate our meals in a more leisurely fashion and I made a call to my mother, Kieran and Clare. Hearing everyone's voice brought my mood back into line. Life is going on as normal in the UK and everyone is wishing us well and are monitoring our progress on our website.

I guess I had prepared myself for the ultimate challenge of Antarctica, what I hadn't taken into consideration was for any of my team to make such a huge mistake, so early. Although, I've lost a few heart beats today with Pita, the bigger picture is I must maintain my determination and enthusiasm. I know I can do this.

Friday 8 Dec 06

With the sun beaming through the tent, I sweated really badly, hence soaking my bag again. I totalled about 4½ hours broken sleep, which is better than nothing. With a relaxed breakfast and toilet session, we struck camp and were away at 1100 hours, which was great. With Pita's Achilles being the major worry, we were all really pleased when he did 2.9 miles on the first leg. We maintained the momentum by clocking 12 miles in 4 leads, yesterdays forced rest has produced great benefits. We had considered taking a complete day off but with the weather being so unpredictable, we decided that even if we only managed a few miles in bad weather it would be a step closer to our goal. We completed 15 miles in 8½ hours and then stopped as we'd covered our planned mileage and the guys with injuries could stop and recuperate. With tents and toilet complete, I spoke to Dr John, gave him an update on Pita, all's well as they can be; he's impressed with what we've done and how Pita is coping. Today we passed the 85 degrees line which means we are half way, only 300 Nms to go with lighter pulks, it's a big barrier broken so now we are heading to the Polar Plateau. We have a clear view of the summits of Theil mountains, they do look awesome but will look even better when we can't see them, meaning behind us to our North.

We've had poor communications tonight, so the despatch will hopefully go in the morning. I've felt good today but I'm starting to feel hungry for most of the day, my chocolate and peanuts are only just achieving their aim while "Tommy Tapeworm" grumbles and eats away in my tummy. I'm struggling eating 2 meals at once, but I must persevere, the main worry is, I'll make myself sick, having eaten too much. Potentially we have 18 days to go, so it wont kill me but I could lose at least another 1½ stone, which will be good for the abdominals. The feeling in my fingers is still poor but I think my skin is growing back on my tips. My thighs are a wee bit sore but bearable, as I'm putting Vaseline onto the small wounds twice a day. This evening we had a wee celebratory "half way there" piece of Auntie Elma's Clootie Dumpling. Clootie Dumpling is an awesome cake full of stodge, protein and it tastes bloody wonderful, oh and also by the tastes of it, a bottle of brandy went into it, we are keeping the rest of it for the South Pole, thanks Elma, you are a diamond and are in our thoughts.

Saturday 9 Dec 06

Had a great night's sleep after listening to my MP3 until midnight, it's amazing how the music lets me drift off to warmer climates and happier occasions, probably Auntie Elma's Clootie dumpling had helped too. After a normal start, we set off early at 1030 hours, which was brilliant. The weather was perfect all day with temperatures around – 25 degrees, light winds and clear, bright skies. We cracked on really well, I managed another 2.9 miler up hill, which felt really good, considering I've had a twinge in my sciatic nerve for the past 3 days. It happened while I was digging out the toilet 2 nights ago. I'm taking Ibuprofen and my own painkillers, which certainly ease the pain; I pray that it does not get any worse. I am being very protective not to damage it anymore, I'm sure it will be fine. With the 15 miles covered in 8 ½ hours, we decided to stop and enjoy the rest, which is becoming increasingly important. As I'm only monitoring dates, I'm losing track of days, but thankfully realised it was Saturday. So I made a call to mum, as I knew Clare had taken her parents to see her. Joshua was feeding every 1 ½ hours, crickey Clare must be shattered, making my guilt sink even deeper. But this also gave me the kick up the bum, that I must complete this journey and justify my selfish challenge. It was a lovely thought though, that while I'm out here, my brother Brian was escorting John and Ann with a walk over the Humber Bridge, all our challenges are in perspective. The Humber Bridge also rekindles wonderful memories of my father, so all is good. With Pita on cook, its 2240 hours and I'm chilling out listening to my MP3 so I'm going to try and get some rest before yet another 15 miles tomorrow.

Sunday 10 Dec 06

After relaxing until midnight I slept really well for 6 hours, which was great. I continued with my relaxed mode with Pita being on cook, I got up once the cookers we're on, so the tent felt a bit warmer. This morning I'm cracking open week 5 of food, starting with muesli, which is great (not), supplemented with strawberry Complan. With our tents down, we headed off in perfect weather knowing we had a large climb in front of us. We all had a brilliant day, climbing 500 ft towards the Polar Plateau. I even got my first 3.2 miler in during my 90 minute lead, but the guys discounted it as they reckon I took 95 mins, one day I will get a verified 3 miler, the mickey take is great for morale. The remainder of the day was also excellent. With tents up, I sparked the beacon; it came back 90 mins later with a very good position verification. As my baskets on my poles are broken, I've adopted Phil's idea of cutting a fuel container lid into a basket shape and ramming it on the end of my pole. I hope they work as I need something to stop my poles sinking into the snow, which is really hurting my back. In the past 2 hours, it appears that a storm is brewing which could be quite a toughie. It's the first time since being here that I feel vulnerable as we are so small in such a mass of white destruction. I've been out to check the positioning of the pulks, check the guy ropes and the security of the storm flaps around the edges. Hopefully nothing will come of it but it has rapidly reminded me of the very hostile environment that we have been living in for the past 29 days.

Monday 11 Dec 06
The storm came and created winds of over 80 mph, then incredibly it dropped as quickly as it arrived leaving us thick fog. Being so tired, I slept through most of it but our little anemometer confirmed the wind speed. As I opened our tent door and could see nothing, no contrast but just a small horizon. Fortunately for us, within a couple of hours the sun did its job and burnt it all away. With tents down we headed off into thick whiteout, the person leading could see no more that 2 to 3 feet maximum. During my blind lead through a sastrugi field I thought about the poem "Foot prints" by Mary Stevenson, which concludes with the words, *"When you saw only one set of footprints, it was then that I carried you."* I had given Clare a ring on the day Joshua was born with these words engraved on the inside. I'm not religious but in some strange way these words gave me strength and guidance as I battled my way through this mine field of ice. With no wind and a new layer of snow, we continued into the white abyss for 9½ hours, covering an incredible 12.9 miles. We've had no solar panel source to charge anything, at times the communications can be desperate; hopefully we will get sun tomorrow. It was difficult today, as with no contrast you need 100% concentration, which when mentally and physically shattered is challenging. I don't miss many home comforts but, I would do anything for chunky chips and tomato sauce right now.

Tuesday 12 Dec 06

Another good night's sleep. I think that I'm so shattered after the day's efforts; I'm desperate for rest. Also with no sun radiating through I can almost sleep through the whole night in my bag. Following our normal routine we were off with thick cloud but better contrast than yesterday and a 2 inch cover of fresh snow. Today's temperature is -35 degrees. The fresh snow made pulling the pulk feel like you were pulling it through treacle, especially on the uphill stretches. We continued with our traverse right to avoid the disturbed ice, which works a treat. The guys worked really hard through the latter part of the day to ensure that not only did we complete our 15 miles but also we're now over the 86th degree line, leaving us 240 Nms to go. We quickly set up camp and I got a chance to speak to Clare, Kieran and Mum, as the phone is now fully charged again. As it's overcast and windy, I've got to stop writing this as its –8 degrees inside our tent and I'm freezing with my kit on, that was a first. We're now at a height of 2000 metres that's nearly 2000 ft above Ben Nevis, this is another reason why the temperatures have started to fall.

Wednesday 13 Dec 06

Woke after a good sleep, even though my muscles are a little stiff after yesterday's efforts. After our normal routine we set off at 1040 hours in great conditions of blue skies, light winds and around – 30 degrees. It did take a long time to get my hands and fingers warm, normally they take around 30 mins, but today took over an hour. My thumbs have never been right since day 2, my fingers continue to peel due to the cold. With 13 days to go, I can live with it. We covered a total of 16.3 miles in 9 ½ hours including ascending another 500 ft, which we climbed continuously throughout the day. It really is extremely hard pulling our pulks up hill and through fresh snow, but every step is a step closer. I pulled my first uncontested 3 miler today, followed by a second lead of 1 hour 15 mins, where I covered 2.4 miles. I pushed it out to see how I'm personally going to cope with the 18 milers in 5 days, I can do it but it's going to hurt A LOT. I recognise that I am getting more and more tired each day, but without warning during the day, you can burst into tears, for no apparent reason. Wow, after considering how far we've travelled and how far we must go, I am now realising the immense scale of this challenge, but I know I can do it. Tonight I've been on cook which has given me time to dry out a few things and also find out that the front of my boots are coming away. I've plastered superglue all over them to hopefully stick them. Still the messages continue to flow from all our friends and colleagues (they are amazing), they also included all the latest football results, including the Premiership Table positions. As a Liverpool FC fan, this didn't do a lot for my morale, unlike Phil who supports some crap team called Manchester United, who was very happy. Today, I finally got a chance to open my week 6 card, secret present and chocolates, oh life here, could not be any better. I've actually been sick during the stomach wrenching rides at Alton Towers but no one could have prepared me for the rollercoaster of emotions that Antarctica has dealt me. Although incredibly, I'm thoroughly loving every minute of it, knowing how lucky we are standing on this continent of frozen milk. It's now 2350 hours it's about +20 degrees inside the tent and -15 degrees outside, so I'm going to rub E45 into my sores and get some rest, after having another look at my new Liverpool FC book.

Quote from Kirky's diary *"I keep setting mental goals. My next one is to break the 200 Nms to go barrier, then the 120 Nms, then the 100 Nms; I just want to get there now."*

Thursday 14 Dec 06

With the heat of the sun radiating through the side of the tent, it kept me awake until 0300, I've only slept for 4 hours. I'm pretty bushed but there's nothing else you can do. I boiled up all the water for the troops and set off around 1030 hours, which is ½ an hour early, which is great. We did our standard 6 legs in perfect if not too hot conditions as we all drank everything we had for the first time ever. Each day, we are drinking around 1 ½ litres of hot juice, which for the amount of effort would be nowhere enough if you were routinely working out, but this is where I really benefited from my reduction in drinking while pulling my tyres. I cracked 2.97 miles on my lead, during which I nearly screwed up my navigating, due to lack of concentration, thanks to the boys, they corrected me. Leg 5 followed where Kirky pulled another 3 miler plus out of the bag, I was completely knackered during this leg. I had nothing in me to catch Kirky and Phil up; I was totally despondent and dejected. I was so glad when I saw them both stop in the distance. Leg 6 I picked up a bit but was glad the day was over, covering 16.8 miles our most yet. We had trialled this today, as our 18 milers start on Monday, which we have 9 of before we tick the Pole. I've just been across to Kirky and Phil's tent for a chat and Phil kindly volunteered to repair my boot, it's all stitched and raring to go again in the morning, what a troop. As I took my last look outside, it was virtually white out; the world has totally disappeared. Ironically, this gave me an inner feeling of security as for once I couldn't see as far as the eye can see, fingers crossed it will be clear tomorrow.

Friday 15 Dec 06

Reasonable night's sleep, boiled the water for the troops then we were off at 1030 hours again. The weather was very poor contrast but with little sastrugi we made great progress until the sun burned through during lead 2, making conditions excellent. We believe we've had a wee taster of the final plateau, as for about 20 minutes and for the first time since we started, the surface flattened out. That point is worth comprehending, every day has been up hill and at last the surface is starting to plateau. With a great surface we made brilliant progress until we started yet another ascent. We've really pulled some ascent in the past 6 days; we're now at 2200 metres with the South Pole being at 2830 metres. Most of this ascent will happen between now and 88.15 degrees South. I had a particularly nasty first lead today through sastrugi almost 3 foot tall and uphill. I still managed 2.84 miles, which was respectable. My second leg I managed 1.9 miles in 1 hour bringing our total for the day to 17 miles in 9½ hours. I'm finding with the pace and distance increasing, I'm having to concentrate even harder to ensure that I can keep up with the guys. My repaired boots worked well (thanks Phil), so I know they will get me the whole way. It's incredible but we could potentially be at the Pole in 11 day's time (Boxing Day). We've a lot of miles to go 191 miles to be precise, but I'm starting to believe that we can really do it. It still comes down to weather/luck and health, please let us do it, as we have all worked so hard to reach this point. Bad news is the IPAQ's battery is dead so we've no emails or messages tonight. Hopefully with the sun shining tonight it will recharge the batteries so we can get them in the morning. Kirky and Phil are taking up to 15 attempts per night to get the despatch back to our website, with the satellite signal getting more unreliable as we get closer to the South Pole, the guys are doing an incredible job, they have both got the patience of a saint.

Quote from Kirky's diary *"Once we reach 18 Nms a day, even if we are struggling, we have to do it. It's only 9 days of our lives, just think of the end result."*

Saturday 16 Dec 06

Only 3 hours of sleep, as it was so hot with the sun radiating through the tent. Anyway with normal routine completed, we set off with icy sastrugi, 15 kt winds, sunny and bright conditions with a temperature of around -35 degrees, it was freezing very hard. Phil's binding broke on the first leg but he quickly replaced it with the back up, which is working fine. Every lead today was very hard as and it's been up hill all day. The surface of sastrugi has been a constant grind, as you didn't get more than 20 seconds between each pull, jerk, swerve or complete stop. It's so frustrating not getting a rhythm or pace going. Anyway I pulled a 2.8 mile lead. We finished early and short of our intended 15 Nms as Kirky has hurt his ankle, so we decided to rest it, as we had covered 13.3 miles and heaps of height. We did cross the 87 degree line so we're now left with 178 miles to go in 10 days. I feel with Kirky's injury and Phil's binding, Antarctica wants us to know we're not there yet. I've spoke to her (Antarctica) a lot today, asking her to forgive me for my verbal abuse and questioning her parentage, I think only time will tell to see if she repents my sins.

Quote from Kirky's diary "*I heard a twin otter plane today. It is the first outside human contact we have since leaving Patriot Hills on 12 Nov.*"

Sunday 17 Dec 06

Woke up around 0230 hours as the sun was once again beaming through, it kept me awake for over 2 hours. With our normal routine and we were off at 1030 hours, this time it was a little warmer at -32 degrees, with a hard slippery surface. Once again we hit fields of sastrugi, which was very tiring and jarring to our backs, knees and hips. Phil came across our first bit of downhill, it lasted for about 5 minutes, what an incredible feeling of relaxed easy progress with no sastrugi, God it was bloody wonderful. Only wee snag was we had the exact same height and more to pull back up again, at least the surface on that climb was clean and smooth. I had 2 consecutive leads today, covering 5.9 miles, which I am really happy with. With the 18 milers starting tomorrow, I reckon I'll be ok, as long as I pace it correctly. I know we will have to extend our days of physical work to at least 11 hours, which will be a killer. We've got to cover the mileage and with potentially only 9 days to go, it's going to be very hard work but achievable. Anyway we concluded the day covering 15.7 miles, which is excellent considering the surface we crossed in 9½ hours. The main thing I've tried to do today is trying to keep my fingers and thumbs warm, which has been quite difficult as Pita has been slow and waiting at each break for more than 15 minutes is really making me bitterly cold internally. With Pita on cook, I'm going to give him a hand so he can sort his legs out with new bandages, so I'd better close. I say bandages, as we are now out of new sterile bandages, we are now using the inside wrappers of the gauze packaging against his wounds as everything else we have is contaminated in clotted blood and stinking dead tissue.

Monday 18 Dec 06

Slept well, I had at least 5 hours. Before leaving I got a short call into my COMSEC colleagues Bob Ballinger and Andy Russell at work, it was awesome catching up with them, hearing their voices really recharged my batteries with their jovial banter and great encouragement. Unfortunately following their call, I had the worst day so far in so many different ways, which considering we may only have 8 days left, I guess it's not too bad. The terrain has been awful again and this time it mentally got to me. Although I did 2.6 miles I was cursing and swearing throughout in shear frustration. Phil and Kirky were brilliant understanding my fury, by telling me to *"suck it up cupcake, as it's the same for all of us"* I genuinely love these guys. During the second leg, I helped Pita with his makeshift dressings wrappers around his thighs as they had slipped down to his knee. I knew I had to be careful not to let my hands get too cold, but Pita was struggling on his own. It only took around 2 minutes but during that time of untying his matted bandages and replacing them over his horrifically sore open tissue, my hands were absolutely freezing. Over the next 2 hours I kept my thumbs in the fingers compartment of my mitten but I could only restore the heat and feeling in my left hand, my right hand was numb. We achieved 15 miles, 3 short of our plan in 10 hours but considering the conditions we were all happy with the efforts today. We've possibly got 3 more days of this surface as we climb towards the polar plateau. Now for the bad news, tonight I've confirmed I've definitely got frostbite in my right thumb, I don't think it is deep yet but it's very swollen and darkening in colour. All day I've had a sinking feeling that my hand was bad but now the reality is, I've succumbed to Antarctica. There's not a lot I can do, so I will just continue and be very cautious, I am naturally worried as frostbite can only go one way, which is downhill, but I can handle it. The whole situation with Pita is just adding to my growing frustration.

Today we also crossed 2 huge crevasses, which were at least 15 to 20 ft across and we guess approximately 150 ft deep. We knew by our research that the crevasses were here, so as we approached them I became increasingly worried. Without any hesitation Kirky just went for it crossing this weakened snow bridge with the sound of huge chunks of ice dropping from below the bridge into the abyss below. I was furious as we'd planned to cross it by disconnecting our pulks and then take it one crossing at a time. While expressing my frustrations to Kirky and much to Kirky and Phil's amusement, Phil moved up about 20 ft to my left and also went for it. Regardless what I was thinking and shouting about, those 2 were now on the safe side of the crevasse laughing their heads off. Pita was next, leaving me the final crossing with fears of the weakened bridge collapsing. I very gingerly made my crossing with the thoughts that with no rescue equipment if the bridge of ice was to break, I would fall to my certain death. Once over, I couldn't believe my eyes as I watched Kirky and Phil taking photos of the crevasse which included them sticking their ski poles into the bridge to try and see the abyss below. My heart was in my mouth as I watched them posing for photos. This was the first time since arriving on the ice that I'd been annoyed at Kirky and Phil, but while watching them cracking up with laughter and smiling for their photos, the guys knew what they were doing and it was great to seeing them so happy. Over the next 4 hours we crossed several crevasse fields, which were extremely nerve racking. This was another example that Antarctica is the boss and yes we will adhere to her rules.

Tuesday 19 Dec 06

Not a bad sleep, must have got 5½ hours. Did the same routine, we've had great weather today with temperatures around -30 degrees. We covered 15 miles again in 10 hours, as the ground has continued to be horrendous with large fields of sastrugi and lots more uphill. I knew it was going to be hard between 86 and 88 degrees but this is really serious. I've had problems writing tonight as my thumb is a bit of a mess, as I'm now unable to use it. I've lanced my thumb to discharge the pressure of clear fluid, which relieved the pain immediately; it's black, like it has been hit with a hammer and the pain is excruciating. With 7 days to go, I can do this as long as I'm really careful. Knowing the battery was less than half power, I had a 90 second call to Kieran. I hoped that talking to him would make things OK in my mind with sustaining frostbite. Well it did for the 90 seconds, following which I felt

Antarctica stood up on her hind legs and laughed at me and shouted 2 v 0. What a bitch!

Wednesday 20 Dec 06

Slept well apart from my thumbs aching and throbbing, but now at the end of the day, I've lanced it again which gives me instant relieve. It's leaking lots of weepy blood, which is great news as it still has some life in it. I've spoken to Dr John at Patriot Hill base camp, he's happy with my treatment, as long as I keep it clean, it still looks a flipping soggy mess. We've had another very hard day, managing 14 miles in 9 ½ hours. Pita's fitness is really suffering under the poor conditions. The visibility has been down to 100 metres with more biting winds, with endless fields of sastrugi, it is sole destroying but were still cracking on with the mileage. During the rest between leg 5 and 6, I asked Kirky and Phil to crack on ahead, so they could put the tents up as Pita had fallen so far behind. I had to wait for 25 minutes in temperatures around -30 degrees and for the first time I even put on my down duvet jacket in the day as I was bloody freezing, especially my hands. The idea of jumping up and down to create heat, just doesn't hit the spot down here. Pita and my final leg took nearly 2 hours to reach the tents as he was moving so slowly, unfortunately I never regained any heat back into my hands for the whole leg and have now sustained frostbite in my left thumb, I'm absolutely gutted. With 2 hands affected, trying to protect the weaker hand is now fruitless; I just have to get on with every task, regardless of the pain and severe lack of dexterity. It also means that I had to puncture and dress 2 wounds. As it's a self induced pain as I was puncturing one thumb, the thought of puncturing the other almost made me sick. At times it was unbearable, making me think what Pita had been through the past 5 weeks, although I have no sympathy, as now I have my own battles to contend with. I know Boxing Day is out of reach, with the 28th being a more realistic date. This will depend on the weather and surface conditions. Regardless of my feelings and frustration, I'm giving Pita a hand with cooking, so we can get some sleep before another long day tomorrow. There was some good news, we crossed the 88 degree line, which that leaves us 117 miles to go, I hope the plateau is as good as everyone says it is. Please Antarctica, will you let us at least draw with you?

Quote from Kirky's diary *"ALE said we have recorded the most miles in a day so far out of all of the teams on the ice, which is good."*

Thursday 21 Dec 06

Slept OK until the sun kept me awake between 0200 – 0330 hours, you just have to sleep on top of your sleeping bag. Before heading off, I now empty each sack of fluid to relieve the pressure and tape off the soggy skin with surgical tape. Normal routine then headed off towards the plateau in temperatures of around -45 degrees, with 20 kt winds and very poor visibility, or so I thought. At the end of leg 4, after approximately 14 miles, Pita was struggling and announced that he couldn't go on. We immediately put the tents up, grabbed a brew each and sat to work out our options. It was clear that Pita had given his all but with no antibiotics fighting his infected body, the infection was winning. With several options decided, I phoned ALE to enquire if there was a routine flight in the vicinity that could pick Pita up. They've asked us to divert 16 miles off route to a known landing site, which in my opinion is not an option, as I'd rather head further South and find a site of our own to get him picked up. It has been heart wrenching to make this decision but I know it's the right one;

I'm gravely concerned for the long term effects on Pita. If there's no pick up, regardless of what happens, Phil and Kirky have devised a rolling plan idea, which will mean skiing for 6 hours, resting 6 hours etc. It's a great option as the efforts required would be in smaller chunks that Pita could potentially manage. Although it will be extremely hard, it will provide more rest for everyone and we can bang the calories in as we burn them. This would ensure that we will get there for 27/28th Dec. This expedition will succeed regardless of the abyss we seem to be falling into.

Thanks to Kirky constantly charging the phone battery, I had a wonderful 15 minute chat with Clare which greatly helped me as my self induced pressure which was now building inside me. I made the decision before calling not to tell her about my thumbs as I felt, one it wouldn't make any difference and two, she has enough going on looking after Joshua. I cannot stress how supportive Phil and Kirky have been but I feel they would have seen Pita return to Patriot Hills on day 1. But recognising that he had covered almost 500 nautical miles, I feel that the right decision was made and that it's down to the lack of medication that Antarctica is beating him. Tonight, I've had to relieve both my thumbs of fluid. It's a simple but excruciatingly painful task. I first place my Gerber multi tool knife in the cookers flames to sterilise it, sink the blade into the ice and then carefully puncture my blisters in several locations to release the liquid, which instantly reduces the pressure. Most of the fluid drips away to the ice, but I use my head scarf (Buffy) to squeeze out any last remnants of fluid. I keep the dressings off during the night and then place a medical tape over them in the day to try reducing the inflammation as I don't want the liquid to freeze. Unlike a blister you sustain on an ankle caused by friction, once it bursts, it rarely fills again. The response from the body is for these blisters to constantly refill again. It's messy but knowing I'm in spitting distance of the Pole, I can cope with the pain; anyway, I've nothing else to do.

Friday 22 Dec 06

We woke to 20 kt winds and biting -45 degrees temperatures again battering the outside of our tents. We did our normal routine and set off knowing that now we were on the plateau with minimum ascent today. Knowing we were reverting to our amended plan of 6 hours on, the first leg went to plan covering over 3 miles, but close to end of the second leg Pita collapsed and this time, he couldn't get up. As the winds had strengthened to over 35 kts I struggled to call Phil and Kirky back and then together we put the tent up. Pita looked dejected, confused and like death. While Kirky got the cooker on, I stepped outside into the biting winds and walked around the tent in what seemed like a screaming nightmare. I knew what I had to do, but the reality of saying it was going to destroy me. After a little over 5 minutes, I opened the tent door, sank to my knees, looked Kirky and Phil in the eyes and told them I was aborting the expedition. I felt empty although I wanted to be sick. I couldn't bring myself to look at Pita; I looked away from the guys and burst into tears. Even with the wind howling a gale outside, the silence in the tent was static.

The expressions on the guys faces was numb, our dream was over. Knowing the weather was so bad, the chances of any air drop or pick up was nil. Pita was dying; whatever infection he had was poisoning him from inside and was now probably affecting his vital organs. The silence was broken with Kirky offering hot water for a brew. Nothing anyone said or did, made no difference, all of us had been flattened. After putting the second tent up, I returned to my tent to break the silence with Pita. For the first time in 42 days, we had nothing in common; I was looking at the person who has destroyed my dream. We spoke about his medical condition and that he must drink as much as possible as to help his kidney's and maintain his temperature. I laid on my sleeping bag, making notes about what I was going to say to ALE, as now they were going to be key stake holder as to what happens next. The call to ALE infuriated me as they were clearly not listening as they muttered about pushing on a further 30 miles to the last degree landing site. The hardest part of the call was reiterating to ALE that all 4 of us required picking up, not just Pita. The team had made a pact that if one member was to be removed from the ice, then all of us would leave. Even if we rescinded our agreement, we also knew we only had one phone working and the beacons had been giving us some very spurious readings, not knowing if it was on the easting or westing longitude. Keeping my emotions composed was like piecing together a baked bean jigsaw, but eventually ALE accepted my request and asked for the team to venture out 1 mile to the North, East, South and West to look for a suitable landing site. The major problem was the fields of sastrugi, which would need to be broken down so the Twin Otter could land, but for today, it's not important.

While I was writing this I knew the dream was over, the stress, the sleepless nights that I endured, was for what? But now my priority was really life or death, if we don't get Pita to medical aid, would he die? This nightmare would not be over until we're at Patriot Hills, where Dr John can treat him, which weather depending could be a few more days. On a lighter note, I was wondering as we've chartered the flight, could we still get the opportunity to go to the South Pole. As I laid on my bag with my eyes full of tears, I am completed gutted and numb knowing I won't reach the South Pole by my own steam. I know that Clare and I have a beautiful son, we also have Kieran and I have my family and together we will have a wonderful life ahead of us. To be honest it was the only thing that was keeping me, I was devastated.

Quote from Kirky's diary *"I have cried loads in the last few days, as I've seen my dream slipping from my grasp. I am too upset to keep writing, so will write more later."*

Saturday 23 Dec 06
I hardly slept, which had nothing to do with the winds battering the tent. Every time I rolled over and saw Pita, I rolled back over again, I couldn't bear to look at him as the emotions of bitterness were eating me away from inside. We've

split the cookers so we can brew up and eat as and when we feel like it. Today we have provided 2 to 3 hourly situation reports (sitreps) of actual weather conditions to ALE, as we've watched the weather slowly deteriorate. We have also decided that after reading so many wonderful messages of encouragement on our website that we have had to announce our devastating news of aborting our attempt on the Pole. We first made calls home to reduce the worry of our families and loved ones. Speaking to Clare was heart breaking. It had not only been me who had gone through hell and high water to reach this point, but Clare had experienced all my emotions that had gone through with the endless work. She was as devastated as we all were, but I haven't told her about my thumbs. At the moment it's cosmetic in the big picture, I felt all she needed to know was that Pita was alive and we were looking after him.

At 1200 hours I phoned ALE with another sitrep. He advised me that a Twin Otter had reached the Theil Mountains refuelling point and was waiting for a weather window. I've also vigorously pushed across to Mike Sharp the co-ordinator from ALE that as we had paid for a chartered plane from the South Pole, could he arrange for the pilot to take us to destination of our dreams? As there were so many aspects about the flight to consider, the fuel, our weight with equipment and in particular the weather, the priority had to be to get us back to Patriot Hills, so that Pita can receive treatment. I've decided not to tell the team about my request as it so easily may not happen. With the weather being so poor, there was always the chance that we may not make the Illusion flight on the 29th Dec that will be something to worry about at a later date. For now, my thumbs were thumbs are just a gory mess. My right thumb was now swollen up to the first knuckle. As we are stationary I've taken to puncturing a hole in the base of it so I can relieve the pressure every 4 to 5 hours. It had an array of colours from pasty wax to black, red and purple. The top of the thumb had now split, where I had punctured it so many times and was now dead.

My left thumb has the same characteristics and had one further snag. Once I'd relieved the fluid from the bottom of the nail, it appears that the whole nail had become detached from its foundation and can move from side to side without any restrictions, which was sporty and a little concerning. When I went outside to the toilet the saggy remains of the top of my thumb, got instantly cold as I think the blood supply was becoming very limited. All this aside, I know in my own mind, that with them strapped with surgical tape, I could have still carried on.

Quote from Kirky's diary *"I was at my lowest point that I can remember in life – utterly devastated. It's going to take a while to come to terms with this."*

Sunday 24 Dec 06

Really poor night's sleep. Phoned ALE at 1200 hours, the flight looks like it's on. It's going to drop off a party at the last degree, then vector to our location. Even though that was the plan, we still provided 2 hourly actual weather reports as the cloud base was varying by the hour. We were told that the aircraft could possibly be with us in 2 hours. Ironically within minutes of that call, a deafening roar broke the silence, as the 2 engines of the Twin Otter flew 20 ft above our tents. The next 20 minutes were very tense as we watched with amazement the pilot, Captain Steve try on at least 10 occasions to land his aircraft. He tried various makeshift sastrugi filled runways to land, but each time he put the throttle full on to take off and try again.

I think it was around on his 12th attempt he successfully got the ski under carriage down and stayed down, he had landed and this was our way home. Hearing the engines and actually seeing the aircraft was the first human intervention I had experienced over the past 6 weeks. It was surreal as no sooner did we confirm he had landed safely, we immediately struck camp. During which my thumbs took one hell of a battering, as we realised that if the weather changed as rapidly as it has been doing, we may not be able to take off. The landing site was approximately over a mile away, so together we took Pita's pulk in relays to transport it to the awaiting aircraft. Pita was absolutely shattered and showed no signs of any energy as we slowly escorted him to the aircraft. Once all of our pulks were at the aircraft we then spent the next 90 mins digging our own runway by breaking down the sastrugi. As the aircraft was going to take off with all 6 of us and our equipment, it needed at least 300 metres to give it enough clearance to take off. Personally I found this quite amusing as this was the most expensive element of the whole trip. We had paid £85K for a flight back from the South Pole and we now had to dig our own bloody runway. Please don't ever complain at paying British Airways prices again! After working extremely hard to clear away the sastrugi, we all returned to Pita and the aircraft and buckled ourselves in. Captain Steve turned and faced us all. With a secret saddened face, he said that as he was so far outside his flying hours, he was left with no option. We all looked at each puzzled. He then burst out laughing and said that we best go to the South Pole and get some fuel and tee shirts. I was nearly sick as I sat motionless. We were going to experience our dream. Captain Steve then used the weight of the aircraft to give the runway one final flattering, before he turned into the wind to reach the start of our make shift runway. He then gave us a huge smile, a quick wink of his eye and then put full throttle on with his hand firmly gripping the throttle handle. This was further guarded by Co Pilot Justin who placed his hand behind Steve's on the throttle to prevent either of them slipping. With the brakes off, the Twin Otter catapulted itself into some instant speed and then rattled itself down the ice runway, which we had dug.

What a take off, as we bounced and rattled off one piece of ice to another and then finally quiet, the bird was airborne, I was so relieved. Even though, as you know I am petrified of flying, I had such a multitude of thoughts and emotions filling my head, I never had time for any scary aircraft crash scenarios. The 40 minute flight to the bottom of our world was an incredibly emotional time, as the view of Antarctica was simply breath taking, she is one hell of a continent. After about 10 minutes we buzzed the Royal Marines who were approximately 23 miles ahead of us, I subsequently found out that by us buzzing them at 50 feet was also their first encounter with any outside contact and made the whole episode a very emotional time for them. I found it very difficult trying to describe the view; we were at 200 ft, looking over a mass white expanse of ice, which no human had ever touched before. This was perhaps one of the last places in the world were 99.9 % of its lands are untouched, but we had been so privileged to have shared it for over 6 weeks. I was overjoyed but at the same time, I was breaking down with tears.

As we approached the South Pole base, I was speechless. The communication aerials and buildings that I had dreamt so much about reaching over the past 2½ years was there right in front of me, instead of seeing them from the ground from approximately 5 miles away. I thought back to our meeting with Zoe Hudson back in London, where she had delayed her response as to what it felt like to reach the South Pole. I could now never answer her as I felt I had cheated; yes there was the relief but the feeling of not reaching there on our own account made me feel vile.

We first landed on the blue ice runway that was used by around 360 USAF Hercules flights each year and immediately broke right to the refuelling area to get the aircrafts admin out of the way. How ironic that only now that we were at the South Pole did I find out about the USAF flights, which could have saved us a few pounds and a tonne of work. We initially thought we only had around 10 minutes on site to take some ceremonial photos, but to our amazement Captain Steve, said that due to his flying hours, he now needed some rest. This meant we could take our time and accept the wonderful warm welcome from the base commander Andy Martinez who then provided us a guided tour around his complex. It started with a visit to their eating hall where we devoured coffee and cakes, while sat in an area surrounded by the personnel who work at the Pole for the summer season.

The manner in which we had all suddenly stepped back into a normal way of life was almost transparent but disorientating. 2 hours ago, we were literally surviving on the bare ice of Antarctica, now we were all sat in comfy seats, drinking coffee, eating cakes while watching dozens of people getting stuck in to their Christmas dinner. By the way, the time was now 1120 hours on Christmas Day (New Zealand time). All of this and the next 2 hours seemed almost surreal and completely mind blowing. For example, when we climbed some stairs, our muscles just went into shock, as we had not used this muscle group to climb anything for 42 days, it had been ski, ski and ski. The amazing tour included visiting the large gym, a cardio vascular testing gym, green house, library, a quiet room, computer room, science room, communications room, hospital, dentist, fire station, a massive power generator and a room with the huge tanks that provide the water. There was even a postal room, which to my astonishment, I had a letter waiting for me. In total disbelief, I looked at the envelope that clearly had my name and Exercise Southern Reach on it. I carefully opened it to find out it had been sent by an Italian chap, who for a hobby collected the signatures of all personnel who reach the South Pole. Well, I wrote about the circumstances of our trip but dutifully signed it and returned it to the sender; that was so bizarre.

The complex is one massive set up that is incredibly efficient and professional. To think that everything had been flown there since the mid 1960's was incomprehensible. Further to this, we were advised that the whole complex had been raised around 12 ft, to allow an extension the working life of the building by around 25 years. Although Antarctica is not owned by any one country the United States have got one massive share in what happens down at the bottom of the world. After 2 ½ hours, we finally stepped out of the Scott/ Amundsen dome and proceeded to take our once in a life time ceremonial photographs. Regardless of the circumstances, the feeling was breath taking and a complete honour. To think that Captain Robert Falcon Scott had stood there with his heroic team in 1912, I've been lucky to have experienced so many proud moments in my life but this was just without doubt the very best.

I could see the disappointment in the troop's faces but having the consolation of actually experiencing the South Pole had definitely helped in softening the blow of aborting the expedition some 3 days earlier. Then came my life changing phone call. As we had hammered the phone battery with so many weather updates, there was only 48 seconds of battery life left. I announced to the team my intentions of proposing to Clare and without any hesitations the guys forfeited their quick call to their loved ones to allow me to call her.

As I knelt on one knee, while propped up again the red and white momentous marker of the South Pole, I pressed the green call button. With my thoughts and emotions all over the place I had not recognised that back in the UK it was now 0120 hours on Christmas Day, the female who answered the phone sounded very sleepy. I loudly asked Clare could she hear me to which I think the person said I'll just get her. I was so confused but knowing I only had seconds to spare I just thought I would pop the question, until I realised it was Clare's best friend Jackie, who unbeknown to me was staying at our house. The next thing Clare was on the end of the phone. The conversation went like this:
"Clare can you hear me?"
"Yes, what's wrong, are you alright?"
"Yes I'm fine, I'm at the South Pole, on one knee, will you marry me?"
"What did you say?"
"I'm at the South Pole, will you marry me?"
"Yes"

And then silence, the battery was dead. My mind was like spaghetti, I was sure Clare had said yes, but the phone had cut out. The guys were awesome, while congratulating me; I could see the genuine meaning in their looks. I was so incredibly grateful that the guys had given me the opportunity to use the last 48 seconds rather than speak to their families; I will always owe them my gratitude for life. We next slowly walked back to the plane and strapped in. This time we gracefully took off on the flat runway taking the memories of actually touching the South Pole in our hearts and minds that will remain with us for the rest of our lives.

No sooner had we taken off, Justin opened a wee paper bag and threw some rolls at us, which I must say tasted delicious, I don't remember bread tasting so good, we all savoured every small mouth full. We completed the 5 hour flight back to Patriot Hills via the landing site at the Theil Mountains as Dr John had been treating members of a ladies supported expedition for minor frost nip. With John on board, he immediately got the smell from Pita's legs and said he would sort him out back at Patriot. The look on Johns' face when he looked at my thumbs gave me heart sinking feeling; I think the confirmation of someone like John actually seeing them gave me the reality of what had actually happened. John broke the moment by saying there was only one answer, he did this silently by passing me an opened bottle of whisky which I gratefully shared a dram with him and the team. Even though I was exhausted and now living on adrenalin I spent the whole flight admiring the incredible views of this beautiful continent, I knew I would not be coming back so I had to make the most of this once in a lifetime flight. So much went through my mind, but wondering what was going to happen over the next week was at the fore. As we calmly landed back at Patriot, we were warmly greeted by Mike Sharp and his team, which was yet another memorable moment. The last time we had seen these guys, we were full of adrenaline and determination, now was a different story.

Within minutes Pita and I were in the medical tent. Pita was treated first as he was in a mess. As suspected his legs were now rotting from inside and he was diagnosed with septicaemia. Without question, if we had continued putting his body under such strain, he could have died. Even now, I still can't imagine how much pain he had endured over the past 6 weeks, but thank God he was still alive. With antibiotics in him and his wounds cleaned properly for the first time in weeks, he hobbled back to one of the ALE tents to rest up and start his road to recovery. For me, I had made several calls to several mountain rescue troops asking for advice on frostbite. They concurred that the new approach was to expose the injured area to assess the extent of the damaged tissue. Dr John assessed them and decided to rewarm flush both my thumbs. He explained that it's not good news, both thumbs are badly frostbitten and that I will require some elements of my thumbs to be amputated. Having been at the South Pole only 6 hours previously, this news sobered me up instantly. We considered the options and lightly bandaged my thumbs. He gave me some pain killers, capillary inducers and Aspirin to start my repair process.

Then we were all treated to a wonderful Tandoori Chicken meal as our Christmas breakfast, beer or coffee and as much cake as we wanted, please note the time is now 0630 hours GMT on Christmas Day. This food melted in our mouths and tasted delicious, especially as it wasn't supplemented with bloody pemmikan. With our phone now plugged into a new power source, I then spent the next hour talking to all my family, starting with Clare to confirm she had definitely said yes, she had, yehaaaa. Speaking while sat on a chair from a secure atmosphere, did feel surreal. However, after chatting to all my family, for the first time in weeks I felt safe, alive and almost complete.

After my calls, Mike kindly offered the use of his staff tents, to save us the effort of putting up our own. These tents were huge, as you can stand up in them and they even had a mattress, this was almost glamping at -15 degrees. As I put my head down after being awake for over 28 hours, I do not believe that I will ever experience another day like this. It has held so many mixed emotions, but for now, I can proudly say that I have been to the South Pole and soon I will be returning home to my fiancé and children.

Quote from Kirky's diary – *"We had skied over 500 Nms in 42 days solid, this in itself is a great achievement. After Al had proposed to Clare, Phil, Al and I all hugged each other at the South Pole. Pita had in usual fashion had wandered off – a good thing really as I don't think he would have been welcome in such a close, personal and highly charged emotional embrace."*

Monday 25 Dec 06

I awoke at 1130 hours having only slept for 2½ hours as I was in agony. I took one of Pita's booster pain killers and then opened up all of the wonderful cards and presents that I had planned to open up over the coming week. I found it difficult to describe how I was feeling, although while I was reading my cards, my morale could not be any higher, although constantly my sub conscious gut feeling kept raising its nauseating head. I guess I just wanted to go home.

I then read the final chapter of my book Angels and Demons, which was an excellent read. I then got up and joined the team for a tasty brunch, sharing the table while comparing amazing stories with other great explorers and mountaineers. One great explorer was called Sam Silverstein, this amazing guy was returning to Antarctica after ascending Mt Vincent some 40 years earlier. Mt Vincent is the highest mountain in Antarctica and is one of the 7 highest mountains in the 7 continents.

After 3 hours, everyone went outside to play a game of football on ice. Being cautious I volunteered to work the bar that had been cut out of the ice, ensuring that I kept my gloves on. As Phil had brought his Father Christmas outfit, he volunteered to be referee and did a memorable great job. After the match everyone stood by the ice bar, chatting about his or her adventures on Mt Vincent and Antarctica. As we were being hosted by ALE, when we returned to the mess tent, we were greeted with a great festive set up of laden tables of Christmas cheer and a great feast. I utilised the time before the meal, to speak to all of my family again, to compare how their Christmas days had panned out and what their intentions were for the remaining hours of the day. Everyone had had a brilliant day, which maintained my morale immensely. Our Christmas meal with all of the traditional trimming was so incredibly tasty after eating dried food for the past 6 weeks. Although there was plenty of beer and wine, I enjoyed soft drinks considering the bleach type medication I was now digesting. The only negative aspect was the effect the fresh vegetables, meat and gravy had on my tummy. Unfortunately the food mixed with my medication only lasted in my tummy for around 4 hours. As my stomach rumbled like a pot of boiling soup, I thankfully made it to the toilet. It was only after the initial relief of making it in time, that I realised I was sitting on an actual toilet with a toilet roll in full view. In my panic to reach the toilet, I hadn't once thought about grabbing my jacket with my marigolds in. At base camp, the human waste is collected under the toilet in bags and is then flown back to the mainland via the Illusion 76. The evening was yet another once in a life time memorable event, which concluded around midnight. Reflecting on the different time zones we had visited, we had experienced a 36½ hour Christmas Day, which for so many reasons will remain with me as one of the greatest days of my life. As I laid in my sleeping bag, for the first time, I felt that the past 2½ years had NOW been worth it.

Quote from Kirky's diary *"ALE were not only accommodating us but feeding us as well. If only they realised how hungry we are. The food was awesome."*

Tuesday 26 Dec 06

I slept for almost 8 hours, with the occasional stabbing pain. I sorted my kit out and headed across to breakfast, very happy that all was well and on track. Then my day took a huge dive. As planned I went across to see Dr John and Simon his medical assistant. When we removed my bandages the thumbs were awful and smelt terribly, as they had now fully re warmed and completely melted. We soaked them in a warm iodine solution and then made the decision to remove the dead skin. This resulted with 3 mm of skin including my nail and nail bed being removed without any anaesthetic to expose the damage under the tissue. In a nutshell the entire lower segment of my thumb nerve endings had died. My right thumb had virtually no blood supply to the bone but my left had a marginal chance of survival. I brought the troops in to witness how things were, I think it was only when I saw their reaction that it hit me and made the reality of the situation, hit home like a sledge hammer. John had concerns and wanted me to see a specialist in Birmingham. I then spent the next 3 hours contemplating what may happen to my thumbs when I get back to the UK. My mind and thoughts were in deep shock as all I could picture was the mangled ends of my thumbs. Wanting to break my devastating train of thought, I decided to speak to my best mate Steve Cox, who I knew would make light of the situation. I've known Coxy known as "Knob", as we both called each other since 1983, and no sooner had he realised who he was talking to, started taking the mickey immediately. For 10 minutes he had me in hysterics, making all sorts in innuendos about my shortened thumbs, still being longer than my appendage. Coxy was brilliant and was just what I needed. The best news of the day came out when ALE decided to put on a refuelling flight tonight, which will take us back to Punta Arenas. Officially as it was a Dangerous Air Cargo flight, this would not routinely be allowed to carry passengers. However, Mike had amended the manifest and had included the 4 of us as aircrew. I also got Dr John to contact our insurance company to get Pita and I an earlier flight home. Kirky and Phil are happy to stay in Chile to close down all of the admin like showing appreciation to the Chilean Air Force and to sort out our equipment to be sent back by the freight company. They've also mentioned about possibly utilising the spare time before their flights are due to visit Patagonia, well, it would be very rude not to. I spent an hour repacking my pulk for the flight and saying farewell to the friends whom we had only met 36 hours previously. I then spent over an hour walking around the camp, absorbing my last look at Antarctica. She is beautiful, she is dangerous and she will be in my memory forever. Whether I will ever have the honour of returning to see her again, I don't know, but with my frostbitten thumbs and the memories that are lasered into my mind, I will always cherish her in my life.

Hearing and seeing this eclipse sized Illusion 76 land, I knew our dream was about to come to an end. Phil, Kirky and I walked together as Pita was taken to the aircraft by a snow mobile. The 3 of us chatted about our close friendship and how that although we hadn't made it the whole way on foot, we had been to the South Pole, which is what we had set out to achieve 2½ years previously. We shook hands with the ALE team leaving Adam the radio operator and Mike Sharp to last, these 2 guys had both been like our life support machine throughout our stay on the ice. We slowly climbed up the ladders as I took one last glance at her and a huge gulp of frozen air before I entered the darkened fuselage of this beast of an aircraft. We buckled ourselves in to start the next stage of our journey home. The deafening take off in comparison to the landing was so gentle and within minutes the ALE team got up and again made sandwiches for us all before most of the troops took some sleep, as like before, we knew we had 5 hours before landing in Chile. I couldn't sleep; as my mind was now full of "what if" type thoughts. The last time I had been on the aircraft, I was bursting with anticipation and excitement, now I was returning a beaten man, who had almost completed his goal. Would this be how we would be remembered, only time will tell? What I did know was that I was returning to England to be re-united with my family and for now, that's all that really mattered.

Landing in Chile was quite uneventful and as our pulks were being placed into a special hold at the airport, we were clear to leave, without even going through any customs. We were greeted back to terra firma by a very smiley David from CAF, who welcomed our return with open arms before driving us back to the base. I explained to David that Pita and I were booked on an earlier flight home tomorrow, which he said he would happily arrange transport for us. Returning to our rooms, we were reunited with our civilian clothes, towels and wash kit. For the first time in 6 weeks I had a shower. The hot water first felt like blunt needles hitting my skin, but within seconds it changed to a feeling of pure soft silk as it washed away the grime of 42 days of physical exertion. Standing naked in front of the full length mirror, I could see the effects of malnutrition; incredibly I had only lost around 2 stone. After replacing the dressings on my thumbs, I crawled in between the fresh cotton sheets of my bed and sank into a secure deep sleep.

Quote from Kirky's diary *"The hardest part was saying goodbye to Antarctica herself. I know I will be back one day soon."*

Wednesday 27 Dec 06

After waking at 0630, I sneaked another cheeky shower in, as this still felt as some form of novelty before heading for some breakfast at the casino. With 4 hours to go before my flight home, I brought the team together as both Phil and Kirky had requested that they wanted the opportunity to express their feelings and emotions about the events of the past 6 weeks. I must reiterate that throughout the whole time on the ice, the guys had governed their frustrations and had remained completely professional at all times. This meeting allowed them to vent their feelings. The meeting was short but to the point. As the 4 of us sat in a single man's sized bedroom, around 10 ft x 10 ft the atmosphere was tenser than that of an electrical storm. I asked who would like to speak first. Very calmly and softly spoken, Phil broke the silence. While directly looking at Pita, he questioned his integrity, he questioned if he comprehended the results of his mistakes, he portrayed how selfish he had been and commanded that he better not ever go near him again in the UK, or he would not be responsible for his actions. Phil then serenely turned to me while shaking my hand and sincerely thanked me for giving him one of the greatest opportunities of his life. Phil concluded by politely asking me, if he may leave the room. Without a second's hesitation, Kirky asked to speak next. Again, he turned to Pita and said that he agreed with everything that Phil had said including the part of never sharing the same air as him. He went on to add that his arrogance was beyond contempt. Kirky then calmly turned to me, shook my hand and reiterated Phil's sentiments of his experiences he had shared on the ice, then turned and walked out of the room. Looking at Pita, whose face was emotionless, he replied that he felt he was being used as a scapegoat and that their comments were unjust and uncalled for. In complete disbelief, swallowing every ounce of dignity I had left, I stood up and calmly walked out of the room in disgust. I walked outside into the cold Chilean air to break the atmosphere off my clammy skin,

I could not believe what I had just heard. This was going to be some journey home over the next 36 hours. With our bags packed, David arrived and took the 4 of us the mile across the airport to departures. Saying goodbye to Kirky and Phil was filled with so many mixed emotions as this for me would be the end of Exercise Southern Reach the baby I had nurtured for over 2½ years. I also felt guilty that I was leaving the guys behind the reality of preparing all our stinking equipment for its surface journey home. Saying that I knew that these tasks would be softened with their planned visit to Patagonia for a few days. I must admit I had tears when hugging both the guys, but I knew that when they returned to the UK, I would be reunited with 2 adopted brothers who I will be friends with for life.

Conveniently the booking in desk could only put Pita and I together for the first short flight to Santiago, the long haul flights to Miami and then London we were separated, maybe someone was looking after me after all. With hardly a word spoken between us during our first flight, we very quickly caught the connecting flight to Miami. Here we had a 12 hour wait, utilising the comfortable waiting area of one of the airports top hotels. During our time, I changed my bandages in the toilets, as fluid had seeped through to the outer layer. My thumbs are very sore and look horrific. With clean bandages, my thumbs now look tidy and will be as smart as they can be for when I meet Clare at Heathrow. The flight between Miami and Heathrow passed incredibly quickly, as my thoughts fell back on to what we had actually achieved, the mess of my thumbs and but mostly how would the reunion of seeing Clare be? Even though I was unbelievably tired, I hardly slept. Having travelled for 34 hours, today is now the 29th December.

Friday 29 Dec 06

At our flights arrivals baggage carousel, Pita and I stood awkwardly together waiting for our bags to appear. After collecting them, Pita and I made our way through to the arrivals and said our farewells, in comparison to saying goodbye to Kirky and Phil, this was a complete non event. As he disappeared into the crowded airport, I actually sighed a breath of relief; he could now sort himself out. With my heart racing at ten to the dozen with excitement and proudly wearing my dayglow expedition jacket I thought I would be easily recognisable for Clare to spot me. This wasn't the case, as after standing around for 15 minutes I asked the arrivals desk to tannoy Clare, asking her to meet me at the recognised "meeting point". Within seconds, all my dreams and wishes had come true, stood in front of me was Clare holding Joshua. I held them so tightly like I was never going to let them go again. As we separated I then noticed that Jackie, Clare's best friend, the lady I had almost proposed to from the Pole was also with us. What an amazing reunion. Then the question I had been dreading, as Clare looked down at my hands and asked about my bandages. Wow little did I know that another life changing chapter was about to happen.

To conclude the expedition, I feel so proud that having started my mountaineering as a child in the 11th Grimsby Scout Group in the knee deep peat bogs of the Peak District's Kinder Scout and Bleaklow. I have now lived on our 5th largest continent of Antarctica for over 6 weeks, so I can say honestly without any doubt that I have travelled from the Peaks to the Pole.

Expedition equipment laid out at RAF Halton.

Practising putting up our tents in Chile.

	AIR TEMERATURE IN CENTIGRADE											
	5	0	-5	-10	-15	-20	-25	-30	-35	-40	-45	-50
	EQUIVALENT WIND CHILL TEMPERATURE											
5	4	-2	-7	-13	-19	-24	-30	-36	-41	-47	-53	-58
10	3	-3	-9	-15	-21	-27	-33	-39	-45	-51	-57	-63
15	2	-4	-11	-17	-23	-29	-35	-41	-48	-54	-60	-66
20	1	-5	-12	-18	-24	-30	-37	-43	-49	-56	-62	-68
25	1	-6	-12	-19	-25	-32	-38	-44	-51	-57	-64	-70
30	0	-6	-13	-20	-26	-33	-39	-46	-52	-59	-65	-72
35	0	-7	-14	-20	-27	-33	-40	-47	-53	-60	-66	-73
40	-1	-7	-14	-21	-27	-34	-41	-48	-54	-61	-68	-74
45	-1	-8	-15	-21	-28	-35	-42	-48	-55	-62	-69	-75
50	-1	-8	-15	-22	-29	-35	-42	-49	-56	-63	-69	-76
55	-2	-8	-15	-22	-29	-36	-43	-50	-57	-63	-70	-77
60	-2	-9	-16	-23	-30	-36	-43	-50	-57	-64	-71	-78
65	-2	-9	-16	-23	-30	-37	-44	-51	-58	-65	-72	-79
70	-2	-9	-16	-23	-30	-37	-44	-51	-58	-65	-72	-80
75	-3	-10	-17	-24	-31	-38	-45	-52	-59	-66	-73	-80
80	-3	-10	-17	-24	-31	-38	-45	-52	-60	-67	-74	-81

WIND SPEED IN METRES/SECOND

Low risk of frostbite for most people	Risk of frostbite within 30 mins	High risk of frostbite within 5-10 mins	High risk of frostbite within 2-5 minutes	High risk of frostbite within 2 mins or less

The wind chill rapidly increased the susceptibility of frostbite.

Our communications kit includes a beacon, camera, Nokia satellite phone and PDA.

One of my proudest moments of my 31 year RAF service; Putting a team of RAF troops on Antarctica after so many people said it couldn't be done.

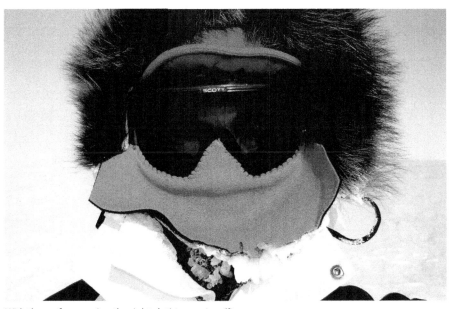

With three of us wearing the right clothing, we're off!

Sometimes, finding a campsite was a little tricky in this pond of frozen milk.

Early days. We were still building wind breaks, but this stopped around day six!

The fully laden pulk weighs 115kgs.

Daily mileages had to be achieved to avoid falling behind schedule.

Sastrugi look so beautiful but are as hard as concrete and challenging to traverse.

Striking out! The sky is blue and on days like this Antarctica is a truly beautiful place.

Melting ice to provide 12 litres of water. The black plastic bag holds an endless supply of water, when you have a working cooker!

Phil building a 5-Star Barratt home toilet! Temperature -40 degrees C.

Kirky surveys one of the many treacherous crevasses we would encounter on our journey.

In the aftermath of our expedition to reach the South Pole, we break down the sastrugi field so "Captain Steve" could take off with six people and all our equipment.

Loading up the Twin Otter for our flight to the bottom of the earth.

Al by the commemorative Amundsen/Scott sign. Robert Falcon Scott's words seem particulalrly apt...
"The Pole. Yes, but under very different circumstances from those expected".

Kirky and Phil, my adopted brothers in arms at the South Pole.

Proposing to Clare on Christmas Day from the South Pole. That has to take some beating, gentlemen!

The proud team with the RAF ensign at the end of an epic adventure.

Christmas Dinner 2006 at the South Pole. A day that I will treasure forever.

Iain Kirk (top left), Phil Mainprize (top right) and me after 47 days on Antarctica.

Income	Amount	Expenditure	Amount
Total Personal Contributions	£8,000	Solar	£20
		Batteries	£15
Public Travel (Flights)	£4,400	Cooking Fuel	£140
RAF Sports Lottery	£5,000	Equipment (as per list below)	£16,795
RAFAT Training Grant	£4,000	Freight outbound	£2816
		Freight inbound	£856
Public Contribution/ Station Under spends	£23,714	Insurance	£821
Trenchard Memorial Awards Fund	£2,000	Food	£2,536
Nuffield Trust	£5,000	Additional food	£500
SIF Grant for Junior Ranks	£2,200	Food while in Chile	£650
RAF AT Special Projects	£9,000	Accommodation	£168
CILOR	£2,536	Website	£57
Sale of expedition equipment	£450	Camera + SD Card + tripod	£175
		Camcorder	£240
		Various charger leads	£59
SYSIS	£500	Transportation Flights	£4400
Havelock School	£618	Flights to Norway to p/u kit	£208
ESS	£1,000	Travel incidentals	£75
QINETIQ	£5,000	Car hire in Chile	£474
Austin Hayes	£1,000	Fuel for hire car	£89
Babcocks Defence Services	£10,000	Parking	£33
Emberson Family	£300	Antarctica Logistics & Expeditions	£124,050,00
Edward/Heneage School	£50		£715
Lady Getty	£1,000	ALE Excess baggage	
Regiment Fund	£400	Mr Hempleman-Adams accm cost	£22
CinC STC Under spend	£70,000		
TOTAL NON-PUBLIC RECEIPTS	£	Team T shirts + plaques	£110
		Gratitude presents total for all 4 expeditions, pictures, T shirts, chocolates	£210
TOTAL PUBLIC RECEIPTS	£	Phone calls, parking, 75 stamps cards Oversea postage of kit	£73
			£23
TOTAL CASH/GRANT RECEIPTS	£156,168	TOTAL PAYMENTS FROM CASH\GRANT RECEIPTS	£156,168

The final income and expenditure spreadsheet for the Antarctic expedition.

ITEM	QTY	ITEM	QTY
Salopettes	4	Ski poles pair	4
Wind jacket	4	Kevlar pulks	4
Socks including gortex socks	12	Down duvet	4
Next to skins x 3	12	Pulk harnesses	4
Warm layer x 3 thermal jacket	12	Repair kit various	1
Gortex jacks with wolverine fur	4	Cooker MSR with heat converter and spares	5
Over hat	4	Tent Hilleberg	2
Balaclava	4	Spoon and thermal mug	4
Gloves x 4	4	Cooking pans	2
Ski boots pair	4	Pee bottle/water	4
Katanka boot (Inner boots)	8	Roll mat and Thermorest	4
Underwear pair	2	GPS receiver	3
Sleeping bag synthetic	4	Satellite phone	2
Ski goggles with neoprene flap	4	Maps/charts	Various
Asnes skis with binding	4	Fuel bottles	6
Sun block	4	3 Litre fuel containers	20
Sun glasses	4	Rechargeable batteries	20
Camera and film	3	Thermos flask	12
Reading material and diary	4	Solar panel with leads	2
First Aid Kit (Including blister and medical tape)	1	Camcorder with charger	1
Bergen 70L+ (with waterproof liner or plastic bag)	4	Tupperware dish to eat from	4
Compass	5		

Serial No	Description of equipment	Price in £
01	Fur for hoods	559
02	PDA plus solar panel	1,115
03	Hilleberg 3 man tents	1,300
04	2 Pulks	1,755
05	Ski's boots, bindings	4,312
06	Kartankas (inner boots)	500
07	Sleeping bags,gortex salopettes, next to skins, thermo bottles, flasks, 3 layers of gloves, outer mittens,	6,100
08	Fuel containers, repair kit items, rechargeable batteries	142
09	Gortex jackets	762
10	Camera case/thermometer/PDA Case	66
11	Dictaphone	75
12	Wind speed monitor	62
13	Cool bags	10
14	Wax	37
	Total on equipment	£16,795

Equipment list and costs.

Chapter 9
Post-expedition aftermath

29 Dec 06

With our hearts still racing, we sat in the coffee bar in London Heathrow airport as I explained the full impact of the seriousness of my injured thumbs. It was obvious that this wasn't the reunion that Clare and I had planned but together we pieced together a way forward. Bearing in mind the RAF was on Christmas holiday, I phone the duty doctor at RAF Halton as she was covering for High Wycombe over the festive period. As we said our fond farewell to Jackie, Clare and I started a journey that would lead to the next chapter of our lives together. On route I made calls to Mum, Kieran and the rest of my family giving them the news that I was safely back in the UK. On arrival at Halton, my bandages were removed to expose the classic necrotic signs of frostbite. The doctor made several calls and arranged for an immediate appointment at the Selly Oak hospital in Birmingham. The look on Clare's face said words for both of us; we had both so much looked forward to returning to our home in Faringdon to celebrate our engagement and to share a belated Christmas together; instead we were heading up North.

With clean dressings on my wounds, we set off for the 2 hour drive to Birmingham, where we were greeted by a military nurse who processed me through A&E. After a short dispute between the plastic surgery and orthopaedic ward I was eventually admitted onto Ward S4 an Orthopaedic Ward, where the majority of military casualties returning from Iraq and Afghanistan are treated. The roller coaster of emotions over the next few hours almost made me sick knowing that no sooner had I been in the arms of Clare and Joshua, we were once again about to be separated, what the hell have I done?

The welfare and care offered to Clare and I was first class, as was the nursing staff softened the blow as well as they could. My main concern was now Joshua, who needed feeding and looking after. Without fuss, Clare just cracked on sorting out Joshua while I was admitted onto the ward. No sooner had I sat next to the bed, I was connected up to 2 intravenous lines containing antibiotics and vascular dilators to improve my circulation. Within a couple of hours, we met a consultant who examined my thumbs and without hesitation announced that my frostbitten residue would be amputated in the next few days and that I was to remain in hospital until the operation. We both sat, frozen to our seats. As during our journey, I had explained to Clare that frostbite injuries are normally left alone until they naturally debride themselves. Who was this guy and could I present an alternative solution? After speaking to the nurse, the answer was no. During all of this time, Clare was looking after Joshua, who we both agreed now needed to be taken home back to Faringdon to ensure that he did not lose his routine; hey he was only 10 weeks old.

For a few seconds we sat in silence, transparently shaking our heads. We had only been back together 8 hours and already we were to be separated again. With incredibly heavy hearts, we held each other before Clare and Joshua left for home. One small consolation was that we were at least in the same country. What further added to my guilt and heartache was Clare had made a navigation error driving out of Birmingham and ended up on the M5 heading South towards Gloucester. This 2 hour journey had taken over 3½ hours with an exceptionally hungry Joshua complaining in the back. All my dreams of how Clare, Joshua and I would be reunited had been shattered, how much deeper could my bank of selfish credit fall?

30 Dec 06

Having spent the previous evening settling in to the ward with my fellow patients, I felt like a fraud with my little wounds. These guys were seriously wounded with injuries varying from amputated limbs, shrapnel wounds and serious head trauma sustained from various incidents within the Gulf. Thankfully we all got on really well which did help to keep my mind occupied. Waking up after sleeping in a comfortable bed for a whole night for the first time in 8 weeks was lush, until I remembered that I was in hospital. Reveille time is around 0700 hours with breakfast following around an hour later. This morning I met the consultant and various military doctors who wanted to review my thumbs as this was quite an original problem for them. Even though I put a compelling case together to let the frostbite debride itself, the team of doctors were too concerned with the potential infection that may occur. After strongly questioning their decision, I was reminded that although I may currently have a beard and having spent time away from the RAF, I was still in the Armed Forces. I don't think as a Warrant Officer of 24 years experienced, I could have been patronised much more. The decision was made and I would undergo surgery on 3 Jan 2007.

What did soften the blow was while I was on the ice; Doctor John had given me a contact of his civilian friend who was fully tuned up on post frostbite management. As it was around New Year it took me 2 days to get hold of him. We enjoyed a great conversation then came the crux of the chat. Unbelievably my consultant who was adamant about amputating my thumbs was his mentor and as the main man in the chair, his diagnosis was probably the correct one. I was gutted.

Clare arrived just after 1000 hours and we spent the whole day catching up on all the news and events that had happened during my time on the ice. It soon became apparent that Clare's time had passed quite quickly as well, as she had not stopped travelling around the country seeing Kieran and my Mum. Our day past so quickly, but as Joshua was being looked after by Clare's Mum and Dad, we agreed that she should leave by 1600 to start her return journey in the light. During the journey to me, Clare had clocked where she had made her error last night and returned home in under 2 hours.

31 Dec 06

Today Clare arrived as well as lots of my family. This very emotional reunion was one of the huge events I had looked forward to during some of the most gruelling times, while pulling the extremely heavy pulk. Once again the day passed so quickly as I said goodbye to everyone for the last time this year. 2006 has been one hell of a year, it's lived up to so many of my expectations, yet it had concluded with me staying in hospital for Hogmanay. Following another tearful farewell I went back to the troops on the ward to make our own Hogmanay entertainment. The welfare team had been and had issued

2 cans of beer for each patient, regardless of the medication we were all on. Incredibly after only a few sips none of us could drink it. The Royal Marine clocked the reason; we were all on an antibiotic called Metronidazole, which has a horrible reaction to alcohol, making it taste like acid. We further found out, this is what hospitals use to administer to alcoholics when admitted into hospital. Without alcohol we rebelliously entertained ourselves by comparing our injuries. One by one we removed our bandages to expose what damage we had endured. Wow, these guys were seriously injured. I must admit this did make me a lot better as one of the guys with an amputated lower leg, commented that within 3 days I would be part of the amputee club. It is strange how the military sense of humour works. With all our injuries exposed, we were making quite a racket of noise while posing so many questions, until our attention was diverted towards the curtains opening around the bed. The nurse stepped in and went apoplectic as we burst into laughter like a bunch of school children. This made the situation even worse, as she questioned us about cross infection etc. OK, we could see her point and she was right, but for us, we were all hacked off that we were in a medical prison for Hogmanay. Over the next hour, the nurses came in and changed all our dressings, understandably they were very annoyed, however, by the time the clocks struck the top of the hour, we were all friends again. Happy New Year 2007. Heaven knows what it has installed for me, but last year is going to take some beating.

1 Jan 07

Clare arrived after having another night of feeding and caring for Joshua. Already the hours of driving and looking after Joshua was catching up on her, so we decided that we'd sort out a wee shift pattern that Clare would see me for 2 days and then have 1 day off to recover. I must say this worked a treat for my whole stay in Selly Oak, having had so much time away from her; I obviously wanted to see as much of Clare and Joshua as I could. Throughout the day the ward was visited by various senior dignitaries and their families, which I must say went down very well with the troops as they had not been forgotten.

2 Jan 07

This morning got off to a great start as one of the military female nurses arrived back to work after having a well earned break from the ward. Before actually starting her shift she took a wee look around the military patient bays and then stormed off to the nursing station. On meeting the night shift staff, she preceded to rant and rave about putting a tramp off the streets in with the military guys. She went on to say it was obvious that this bloke had deliberately hurt this thumbs so he could receive a free bed and food for the night. The 3 inquisitive faces looked back at her with blank expressions, not knowing what she was basing her accusation on. She replied by quietly screaming, the patient with a beard and long hair in the far corner of bay 4. The night staff then took great pleasure in explaining who I was and where I had been. Later that morning, as Caroline brought the drugs trolley around, she sheepishly introduced herself and quietly apologised, much to my great amusement.

Without doubt from my experience these nurses both military and civilian are the best in the world. On occasion they can be treated so badly by some very unruly patients, but they always reply with a smile and a positive attitude. I have nothing but my utmost respect for them all. Starting the new 2 days on, 1 day off pattern, Clare arrived thinking that as I was being operated on tomorrow, so she would take tomorrow off. During the morning we both met the specialist hand surgeon who would be carrying out the operation. This was an incredibly strange conversation, as he spent most of the time talking to my feet. After asking me questions regarding my fitness and whether I smoked or not, he wanted to know what my aspirations were after having the surgery. I explained that I wanted to continue mountaineering, climbing and if financially viable I would like to return to Antarctica to complete the final 91 miles. While still talking to my feet, he asked if I fully recognised the importance of having a thumb. He emphasised that 65% of what we do with our hands is co-ordinated by our thumb. For example fastening a button, pulling up a zip, fastening a belt, writing, tying a shoe lace, driving etc. you name it you use your thumb. My thoughts were immediately fixed on fastening up my climbing harness, tying knots in ropes, placing climbing equipment etc.

Then came his earth quaking offer. He said that he could remove a proportion of my big toes, rebuild replacement toes from my pelvis and tummy tissue and then transplant the toes onto my thumb. The surgeon explained that he had performed the surgery many times before on patients who had sustained industrial injuries with an 85% success rate. Furthermore, he claimed that I would be walking again within 5 days and would probably be climbing again within 18 months. Clare and I looked at each as if there had been a bolt of light appear at the end of a very long tunnel. The surgeon left us to consider the options but advised me that if I wanted this option, he would need to know by first thing tomorrow, to obviously stop the amputation. Clare and I spent the remainder of the day chatting about the various options but every time the subject came back to the fact about the 65% use of your thumb. If you are thinking that the percentage is high, gentlemen please try going for a wee without using your thumb and ladies trying undoing your bra or remove your jewellery, it's virtually impossible. By the time Clare left, my mind was already made, I was going for it.

4 Jan 07

This morning I was visited by my great friend and work colleague Bob Ballinger. It was surreal catching up with him again, as Bob as a very keen mountaineer had followed our progress daily via our website with a keen eye. His description of me made me chuckle, as he walked into the ward and said I was looking like the shell of a man with a mouth and 2 eyes, hidden by a beard, I guess I have lost a bit of weight. Luckily to help my weight loss, Auntie Elma had sent me a red cross parcel so for the first hour, we sat eating her cake, what a superstar, they were delicious. During Bob's visit, we went down to the surgeons ward to assess some photos from a previous toe to thumb transplant. Wow this guy is a magician, although the photos were very explicit, the final result was outstanding. One additional factor that came out during the conversation with the surgeon, was that this would be the world's first ever attempt at a double toe to thumb transplant. My mind was now fully made up and once I had spoken with Clare on the phone, I let the surgeon know that it was all systems go. He then advised me that he planned to bring 2 trainee surgeons over from Asia to observe the operation while it would be simultaneously filmed for other surgeons to learn from in the future. I was more than happy as I would be climbing again in the next 18 months.

8 Jan 07

Today was the big day, I had seen Clare the day before and we knew that the next time we saw each other would be the beginning of a new episode. As per every operation, I was nil by mouth until the anaesthetic team arrived asking me lots of pre-operation questions, followed by being taken down to theatre, where I met the team. As I was already loaded with 2 entry points into my body there was no need for anymore cannula's to be put into my veins. Minutes before I was put to sleep I signed the necessary administration required giving permission for the operation to proceed, followed by giving a small interview on camcorder to the medical team while in the pre theatre room, with my thoughts and feelings. I must admit I was full of confidence as the roller coaster of emotions that had preceded the operation over the past few days was finally coming to fruition.

10 hours 30 mins later, I found myself in the recovery room, really confused and feeling completely off my head, the great thing was though, the operation was complete. As I was on a vascular dilator to open up all my veins and arteries, my blood pressure had dropped so severely that I had to be moved into intensive care. Being so unaware of my surroundings, it must have been almost 2 hours before I realised that both of my arms and both legs were paralysed under the medication and that my condition was far serious than I had anticipated. I remember the one to one nursing staff, encouraged me to eat a sandwich, which created an incredible pain in my throat. As I was unable to move, I was petrified that I had something wrong with my neck as it felt that I had a needle of some sort in there. The nurse explained that the team had tried to establish a cannula into my carotid artery in my neck but had failed so I now had 4 entry points, 1 arterial in my right collar bone area, 1 arterial in my groin and then 1 venial line in each arm. I had a total of 19 lines into my body, with my bed completely surrounded by drug distributors, some making noises and others just hanging off drip hooks. I was in such a mess, but with so much medication dripping into my body, I was too confused to enable me to concentrate for more than a few seconds. After a little while, I was fed the sandwich and fell back into a deep sleep. The next memory I have was of me hallucinating, seeing snakes falling through the air conditioning vents, while a huge raging bear jumped on the end of my bed trying to pull my finger nails out. The nurse was magnificent, by calming me down and filling me with heaps of reassurance. I realise now that as I have never been administered with any drugs of this type before and it was certainly taking its effect both good and bad. The remainder of the day was much of a blur, but knowing that Clare and my family had been phoned, they knew I was safe and out of theatre. From Clare's point of view, she had had a horrific time. The operation was only to

have lasted 6 hours and she had been phoning every hour, only to be informed that there had been complications and that I was still on the slab. When Clare received the call advising her the operation was over, she sighed a relief, only then to be told, I've been put into intensive care and my condition was critical. There was nothing Clare could do apart from worry and visit me the next day.

9 Jan 07

After a night of little sleep and lots of hallucinations of various animals tearing away my hands and arms, I was visited by my surgeon who removed my bandages to reveal my newly extended thumbs. In my semi comatose state I remember seeing my hands but being paralysed from the shoulders down I had no feeling in them, at all. After assessing both thumbs, I was advised that I would need a further operation on my left thumb as the circulation was poor; this operation was assessed to take approximately 90 mins. I think it was apparent that as my body was still acclimatised to the -35 degrees of Antarctica, my veins and arteries were so much smaller than usual.

That morning, I received a visit from one of my bosses from work. The effects of the drugs were incredible, as no sooner had my nurse said John Tapping is waiting to see you, I nervously explained to her that he didn't like me and that he was going to hurt me. The nurse tried reassuring me that he wouldn't have come to see me if he didn't like me, to which I took a 180 degree thought and said, oh maybe it's that I don't like him. Anyway John was stood behind the curtain out of sight, laughing his head off, saying that even after my operation; I must have kept my sense of humour. The thing was John and I are great friends, but the drugs obviously misted my judgement. As he walked through the curtain, I don't know whose reaction was worse, John or mine. John's look was of disbelief. The last time he had seen me was the 1 November, now I laid in front of him as this bearded skeleton being kept alive by so many lines of drugs. John made light of the situation and soon cracked the ice with updates on work and life in general. Shortly after John's departure I was aware that Clare had arrived. The nursing staffs once again were outstanding. Before entering the room, they briefed her on what to expect and the effects that the drugs were having on me. As she walked in, we both burst into tears as the shear mass of medical instruments, drugs and monitoring equipment was over powering. I couldn't even hug or hold her, I was bloody paralysed. How could I have been so selfish to even firstly attempt the South Pole never mind agree to an operation of such severity? As I tried to hold myself together Clare said that she had driven up with her Dad John, who was waiting outside. As John walked in, it was if he didn't know where to look first, then with his very distinct Southern Wiltshire accent said *"Hello Al, how's it going?"* I remember just bursting into laughter and saying *"great mate, do you fancy a pint?"* I was so glad John was there as this must have been such a harrowing sight for Clare to contend with. The day past so quickly but before leaving Clare fed me my first hot meal. I was no better skilled than that of our 11 week old son Joshua. I was at the mercy of anyone who could feed me. Just when I thought I could not have lost anymore self-esteem, after Clare and John left, I needed my first poo. Again the nursing staff were awesome, for them this was routine, for me, I was completed distraught; I had lost every ounce of my dignity.

As the drugs continued to flow into my blood stream, I drifted off into a deep sleep only to wake some many hours later.

10 Jan 07

Awaking as a nil by mouth patient, rapidly reminded me that I was to visit the operating theatre again that morning. As the anaesthetist team talked about the plan, we jovially realised I was not in a position to sign the forthcoming operation consent form, within minutes I drifted into another lovely deep anaesthetic sleep. The operation took over 5½ hours during which the team transplanted some blood vessels from my left wrist and forearm then re-plumbed my left thumb in hope to try and improve the circulation. While waiting in the theatre recovery room, I believe quite a lengthy discussion took place between the S4 orthopaedic ward and the plastics ward again to decide which ward would be most appropriate for me to be admitted onto. S4 won the battle and I was admitted into a side room where I could be closely monitored as my medication had been reduced down to 11 intravenous lines. That night my best mate Steve (Knob) and his lovely wife Debbie came to see me, giving Clare a break from all the travelling that she had been doing over the past 2 weeks. Shortly after they arrived with the mickey being fluently taken I felt the after effects of the anaesthetic making me slowly sink into my pillow. Over the next couple of minutes, bit by bit I felt my body closing down into a complete paralysis, which was scaring the hell out of me. With my oxygen mask on full flow, I tried to shout out to Coxy for help, who was busy claiming that I was a flipping light weight and that I had no appreciation of how much he was missing his take away curry. As my body was rapidly closing down, I couldn't speak loud enough for either of them to hear me. Now, about 3 minutes into this paralysis, Debs noticed that I was mumbling, so Coxy leaned forward to see what I was saying. All I could muster now was *"help"*, to which Coxy replied, *"bloody typical, he just wants more attention from the sexy nurses, I'll see if I can find a bloke!!"* The nurse came in, took one look and called for the anaesthetist team, within seconds a team of 4 doctors arrived and proceeded to prod and probe, throughout which I had no feelings in my body. After showing grave concern, they called for the crash team, following which another 4 doctors turned up. All I could think about and kept telling Coxy, was that I wanted Clare and I'm bloody dying. Things turned even more serious, when Coxy and Debs were asked to leave the room, Christ this was it! I remember the team pulling out a line at a time to see if it made any difference and then I fell into a sleep, which was probably me falling unconscious. Then all of a sudden I felt a rush of excruciating pain in my toes and then my legs, the throbbing blast of adrenaline overpowered any thoughts of dying; now I was in agony. Over the next 20 minutes, much to my immense relief, the doctors plumbed all my lines back in, paralysing only my arms and legs again. Throughout all my years in mountain rescue I've been scared many times, but nothing in comparison to this experience. The only explanation the team gave me was that one of the drugs that I was intravenously receiving had leaked into my central nervous system and that it had temporarily closed down my body. I don't know who was more relieved me or Coxy as now he could leave with Debs to drive home and enjoy a spicy curry instead of driving to Faringdon to give Clare some bad news.

10 - 14 Jan 07
Over the next few days I remained in the side room, while all my wonderful visitors kept up my morale, while the nurses kept topping up my drugs and feeding me my 3 meals a day. I regularly had checks on both my thumbs to ascertain whether the blood was still pumping to the extremities or not. Then came the great news, the doctors had decided to reduce my medication, so Debbie, one of the pain specialists, within minutes removed the taps from my right shoulder and groin. I couldn't believe the length of the pipe which she

removed from my chest, it must have been at least 8 inches long, but what a relief to have them both removed, leaving behind just the two taps in my arms. To ensure I was kept warm and to keep my body flush i.e. constantly sweating, I had a 5ft heater placed above me 24/7, which as you can imagine with my beard and long hair became very uncomfortable. Also I was tired of being called Uncle Albert from the comedy sitcom Only Fools and Horses. After only 2 days, I finally gave in and persuaded Clare to bring my hair clippers into hospital to revert me back to my clean shaven face with a No.2 haircut. With all my hair removed the whole shape of my face changed. One minute I looked like an explorer from the South Pole, to someone who had been a victim in a WWII concentration camp. It scared everyone including me, how my facial expression could change so dramatically. I looked so gaunt with my cheek bones protruding. Even my surgeon walked in to see me later that day and immediately turned around as he thought he had walked into the wrong patient's room.

15 Jan 07

With my new physique and appearance, I may not have looked better but certainly felt heaps better and was determined to get back on my feet. The physiotherapist visited me that morning and arranged for a wonderful nurse called Sergeant Debbie Meikle to help me stand up. Debbie and the physio worked wonders and actually got me standing with support of a gutter Zimmer frame, followed by taking my first 5 steps, which took over 25 minutes to achieve. This to my surprise was an incredibly emotional moment, as I had not moved for over a week. Once stood up, I couldn't actually move my legs; I was bloody petrified with pain shooting from every joint, with both her hands around my ankle, she physically lifted my right as I took my first step. Thinking back that I'd just managed 509 miles in 42 days and now just one single step was a mammoth achievement, certainly put things into perspective. That evening my surgeon removed my bandages for the first time to reveal that both the transplanted toes had very poor circulation. He advised that the surgery team would have an exploratory look on Wed 17 Jan 07, to either improve the circulation or amputate the transplanted toes completely. Looking at them from on top of the hand, they actually looked ok, but as I turned over my wrists, it was obvious that the blood was struggling to perforate the tips, unfortunately, both toes were dying.

16 Jan 07

Today, Clare and I had a heart to heart, trying to piece together what may happen to us over the coming year. This was certainly not what either of us had planned and all thoughts of travelling with Joshua and all of the other things we had both dreamt of over the past 3 months were rapidly disappearing in front of our eyes. Clare is so inspirational, giving all what we discussed a positive aspect; then again if you consider what she has had to endure over the past 3 years, she is an amazing lady. Realising that I had another operation tomorrow, we said our farewells, knowing Clare could take a day's rest from driving. We also knew that regardless of how the operation went it was going to lead us in one direction or another.

17 Jan 07

I had a pretty restless night, as every time I awoke, I could see my nil by mouth sign. I think I'd just gone with the flow with my first 2 operations but this one I was actually quite nervous about. I was second on the list for the morning operations, so after being wheeled down to the pre theatre room, I once again met the surgery team, this time with looks of horror as with no beard or hair, they could see the price of what 6 weeks in Antarctica and 3 weeks in hospital can cost. I drifted off into another deep sleep and awoke only a couple of hours later, feeling very groggy to be told that the team had been left with no choice but to amputate both my transplanted toes. I don't think it immediately sank in, as I fell asleep again in tears, still recovering from the effects of my 3rd general anaesthetic in 10 days. The next thing I remember, I was being pushed along the corridor back to Ward S4, with the nurse reassuring me that the team had tried everything to recover my transplanted toes. I think it must have been the shear emotion of it all but I laid there empty, motionless, crying thinking that the dream of having normal thumbs had vanished. In good military fashion, by the time I had returned to the ward, I'd dried up and composed myself before seeing the guys. After regaining full consciousness, I phoned Clare, Mum and my brothers to tell them the news. Breaking the news was terribly upsetting as it felt that I had let them all down again. If telling them I had aborted the expedition wasn't bad enough, I was now advising them that I didn't even have it in me to play my part in transplanting my toes. All of their kind words really couldn't console my thoughts; my frustration was unbearable but tomorrow would be another day and the start of another chapter.

18 - 23 Jan 07

Over the next week, I was so fortunate to receive literally dozens of visitors. I had always been on the other side of the fence where I was organising the visits to injured troops and breaking my back to make sure their time in hospital was as painless as possible, this time I was on the receiving end. I had almost a conveyor belt of friends, family and troops visiting me, with Clare being my complete rock throughout the whole time. I only found out subsequently that, the troops were not only visiting me, but were leaving masses and I mean tonnes of messages of support to Clare. The support system which I had not seen for so many years, had gone into action transparently, everyone's support was simply outstanding.

24 Jan 07

Today was the day that both Clare and I had been so much looking forward to. With my multitude of medication, a light weight wheel chair, a set of crutches and one huge smile of my face, I left Ward S4 and at long last took the final leg of my incredible journey back to our home in Faringdon. Having said all my farewells and showing my sincere appreciation to all the magnificent staff at Selly Oak hospital, with every ounce of strength I could muster, I walked unsupported from the nurses' station to the entrance doors of the ward, some 40 odd steps, the feeling was flipping awesome. Having passed through the doors, I immediately collapsed into my wheel chair completed exhausted but totally exhilarated knowing we were on our way home. As Clare pushed me down the narrow footpath back to the car park, we almost found ourselves dropping into a 3 foot ditch; both of us were almost hysterical with laughter, feeling the tension fall off our shoulders. Once in the car, we just couldn't stop talking and wondering what we were going to do next. The 2 hour drive passed so quickly and then finally we took the last couple of turnings before seeing our wee palace, which I had thought so much of seeing during my time on the ice. The 20 step walk to the house was agony as I had stiffened up and now I was asking my legs to do it all again. Stepping into our home, I was virtually speechless and overcome with emotions as at last I was safe and back in Faringdon and in almost one piece.

Seeing Joshua just over 3 months old, laying on the rug, so innocent, so perfect was just so surreal. All of the thoughts that had gone through my mind at the lowest times on the ice and in hospital were now all in front of me. Even just sitting down on the settee, changing the channel on the TV, drinking a brew (even through a straw, as I couldn't hold my own mug), having Clare in sight was just unbelievable and breath taking. For that split moment in time with the tears flowing down my cheeks, I felt all the pain and suffering had been worth every minute. It's inconceivable how the mind works.

25 Jan - 7 Feb 07

The priority now was to see my Mum and Kieran, even though I was virtually confined to a wheelchair, being released from hospital would not be complete without seeing them both as soon as possible. 3 days after getting home, I doubled up on my painkillers and nerve blockers and sat in the car for just under 4 hours, as Clare drove Joshua and I to Grimsby to see Mum. Unbeknown to me, my mother had been very poorly over the festive season with another outbreak of cancer. So seeing her beaming smile and receiving her Horlicks warm feeling hug that no one other than your mother can give you, was priceless. I only found out later that year just how poorly Mum had been. We only stayed 1 night, as I was trying to hide my condition, while unbeknown to me Mum was also obviously trying to hide hers too, hey it must be a Sylvester thing! While in Grimsby we also visited my brother Brian's family so I could thank them for their help publicising the expedition while on the ice. I found out after I had aborted the expedition, they had all, including my niece and nephew become famous on TV, giving interviews to both the BBC and ITV.

Coming out of Selly Oak had now created a problem, as I was in need of daily medical support to change my bandages and maintain the copious amount of medication I was taking. As I lived only 8 miles from RAF Brize Norton it made sense for their medical team to look after me, rather than travelling the 47 miles to RAF High Wycombe. This was all approved behind the scenes and I established a great relationship with the medical team at Brize. The support from both the medical and transport section was second to none, as I was unable to drive, I was regularly picked up and taken to and from home, to receive my treatment. I don't know of a comparative service that is available in civvy street, I was so lucky and grateful; the support from the RAF was outstanding.

8 Feb 07

Today was another day that I had thought so much about over the past 3 months. While we had been away on the ice, 2 troops from the office I worked in, Andy Russell and Bill Boshell had volunteered to organise our official home coming party. This included inviting our Patrons, sponsors, senior RAF representatives and of course our families. After waking up around 0600 hours, I couldn't believe that the whole of the UK had come to a virtual standstill as approximately 6 inches of snow had fallen during the night, over the whole country. After a multitude of phone calls from Bill, it became apparent that Kirky was stuck in Aberdeen, Phil was stuck across at Honnington on the East coast and Andy Russell was stuck only 25 miles from High Wycombe. In good old RAF tradition, the show had to go on, so at 1000 hours we confirmed to go ahead with luncheon and the presentation.

As Clare had been called into work at short notice, the transport section at High Wycombe very kindly picked me up and brought me to the camp. On arriving outside my works building I was greeted by 2 of my senior officers who helped me through the snow and up the stairs to my awaiting work colleagues. This was brilliant, just to see their smiling faces and to share a brew with them as if nothing had actually happened, was just perfect. I was now back in reality with a team of guys, who had been so amazing while covering for me at work for over 2 years. Then the bad news, Kirky who was stuck in Aberdeen had our expedition presentation and as it had been produced on an RAF computer, means there were mountains to climb to actually send if over the RAF network. Over the next 90 minutes the guys, re-jigged and re-built an amended version of the presentation, but we had got it. Then it was onto the Officers mess, to meet our awaiting guests who had managed to successfully battle through the snow. The most ironic part of the day, was out of my 4 man team who had been to the South Pole, 2 of them were marooned and at least 12 of our invited guests were either stuck on route or stuck at home. We started the proceedings with Pita and I providing the recently amended presentation to our audience of people who had actually made our expedition happen. As l was still restricted to only 20 paces and struggling to stand, I completed the presentation while sat on a bar stool, mimicking an image of the old Irish comedian Dave Allen. Thankfully our make shift presentation was received extremely well, with some very complementary words spoken by all and was concluded by our military patron Sir Brian Burridge. Once Pita and I had answered all of the questions we were all treated to a first class 5 course meal, followed by saying our fond farewells as our guests were very conscious of the deteriorating weather conditions. This is where I also said goodbye to Pita. I had not asked about his condition and neither he about me. I bitterly resented him looking so healthy, while I was struggling to even stand on my heavily stitched infected feet.

The evening was concluded with Bill taking me back to the Sergeant's Mess, where to my surprise, I was greeted by around 30 mess members welcoming me back. I think their plan was to get me drunk but to their disappointment, I only managed 1 pint all evening. To be honest, I didn't need alcohol to make me merry, the volume of medication I was taking, compensated for around 8 pints. Waking the next morning, the snow had virtually all melted and it was all systems go. Bill very kindly volunteered to get me to Heathrow airport, to pick up Kieran and complete my family at long last.

9 - 12 Feb 07

The last time I had seen Kieran, was outside Swindon's Great Western hospital where we had been forced to say our tearful farewell only the day before his brother Joshua was born, back in October. We'd booked Kieran's flight during the time that Joshua was due, but he arrived a few days late hence missing his brothers birth. The most important factor was to chat to Kieran before he saw me as not only had I physically changed, but I was also confined to a wheelchair and was high as a kite on my various medications. Meeting him at the internal flights arrival area was so emotional; I had seen everyone apart from my boy. Kieran who was 9 years old was looking cool and trendy, while I'll was looking like a very old decrepit man with tears in my eyes. This must have seemed a strange sight to any innocent onlooker but I didn't care, I now had Kieran in my arms and at last my family was complete. Bill very kindly drove us home back to Faringdon, while Kieran and I caught up on the past 3 ½ months. On arrival back at Faringdon, I had to fight back the tears as this was the first time, I had ever seen both my sons together. During Kieran's stay, I constantly struggled to hold back my emotions as the medication played games with my mind. Unfortunately on one occasion, as Kieran was playing on the floor with Joshua, I was laying down on the settee, curled up in the foetal position in agony; there was nothing either of us could do. This must have been so distressing for him, but he played a magnificent role of sourcing my drinkable morphine and helping me to swallow more tablets to ease the pain. Regardless of the amazing achievement we had completed, having a 9 year old caring for his Dad brings you back to reality with a huge slap across the face. As like all my weekends with Kieran, it passed so quickly. The most important thing was that we had seen each other and he now felt part of our complete family of 4 in the South. Following his visit, our phone calls were so much easier as he could relate to my medical condition as I improved by the day.

13 Feb 07

Today after recovering from having all of my family around me, I fell back down to earth with an almighty bang. Shortly after finishing dinner, Clare answered the phone, following which she passed it to me with a very concerned look on her face. It was the Station Medical Officer from RAF Brize Norton, advising me that he had received by recent blood results and I had tested positive to having MRSA. Methicillin-Resistant Staphylococcus Aureus is a type of bacteria that's resistant to several widely used antibiotics. This means infections with MRSA can be harder to treat than other bacterial infections and can often have serious implications. Having heard some horror stories while in Selly Oak hospital, my heart went into my mouth with dozens of wild thoughts rushing through my mind. The doctor was very calming and explained the dos and don'ts until tomorrow when I could meet him for an urgent appointment. Clare could tell by my mannerism on the phone that something was wrong as this roller coaster had just taken another giant fall. Although the doctor had explained as much as he could, I burst into tears once the phone had been put down. My fear now was for Clare and Joshua and that I must not pass on any infection onto them. Jesus, could I have already passed it onto them and Kieran, what else could this situation throw at us?

14 Feb 07

Well some Valentine's day this turned out to be. My appointment with the doctor was very informative and he guided me as to how I should separate all my towels, washing items and be cautious as to how I handled Joshua, only because of the open wounds. I did have a strain of MRSA but he did not believe it to be the type that could potentially blow my candles out. However, as both my toes and my left hand were still badly infected and causing me a great deal of pain, I would now have to have my dressings changed daily, which was a catch 22 situation. As the new skin could only grow if it was left alone, changing the dressings daily would open my wounds, what a pain in the bum! The best bit of news was that it was extremely difficult to pass it on to Clare or Kieran and they were 99% risk free, which was a great relief. As I was feeling poorly and still restricted to around 25 steps, Clare and I shared a lovely Valentines meal in our home.

16 Feb 07

Being part of the military, does have its benefits, as like all of my previous expeditions, it is mandatory to ensure that you take out sufficient insurance to cover all eventualities, as you can imagine, trying to insure a wee walk to the South Pole, was not an easy task. With the help of our Antarctic company, our ski to the Pole was all covered, but in addition I had taken out another insurance which I believe was only available to the military called PAX +. This company is set up to insure troops serving on duty while overseas in conflict areas or while carrying out any active duty including adventurous training. Unbeknown to me, while I had been recovering in Selly Oak, the staff had helped Clare fill in the required paperwork, to submit my claim for compensation. I must say this very efficient company came up trumps and so a juicy cheque compensating me for the loss of my thumbs and payment for my time in Selly Oak arrived in the morning post. Although it wasn't enough to retire on, it did give Clare and I a wee smile, knowing that we could now pay for our wedding, without having to break the bank.

20 Feb - 8 Mar 07

Another excellent facility that the Armed Forces have on offer to any service person with a medical problem is the use of the Defence Medical Rehabilitation Centre at Headley Court. This centre was originally founded to support wounded aircrew having sustained injuries while being involved in an aircraft crash. Nowadays it is primarily full of troops returning injured from the conflicts in Iraq and Afghanistan. With the great influence of the Station Medical Officer at Brize Norton, the doctor managed to get me admitted into Headley, to start my recovery process. Having MRSA I shared an isolation ward with an incredible guy Major Pete Norton who had been seriously injured while attempting to detonate an improvised explosive device. He had suffered an amputated arm and leg, but what an inspirational character, who I subsequently found out later that he had been awarded the George Medal for his outstanding bravery. This is the type of calibre of person being treated at Headley making me feel very humble with my little but personally effected injuries. Pete and I got on really well, proven by the way we took the mickey out of each within minutes. Both Pete and I were so lucky to be looked after by an outstanding nurse Sgt Jazz Robertson. This stunning, broad speaking Glaswegian soon put both Pete and I in our places as we started to mess around with our bandages etc. Before entering the room, Jazz had to don on a plastic apron and mask as we were both infected, this gave us time to reverse any wrong doing before she walked in. So virtually every time we saw her, by the time she entered the room, Pete and I would be hysterics, after quickly covering our tracks.

I spent just under 2 weeks in Headley, receiving outstanding treatment including daily physiotherapy, occupational therapy and one to one remedial instruction to improve my stability and use of hands. The only down side, was that my treatment was extremely painful and made my limbs continually seep with infectious pus. The decision was made that I would serve my time better at home resting and trying to let my wounds granulate themselves before returning for a second go of physio. I must say, that I approached Headley with totally the wrong attitude as I was all fired up to get back into a running mode and pushing my physical strength to the limits; with my injuries this was totally impossible. In fact, on one occasion as I was working through a session of occupational therapy with a wonderful therapist George Glew, we talked through the implications of heading home for my first weekend break. I was bloody adamant that I would not need a wheelchair, as in my opinion, apart from a couple of open wounds there was nothing wrong with me. So to physically hang me, he casually asked me to walk with him up the corridor which included a small ramp, which was no more than 10 yards. I lasted only 9 steps before I was hanging on to the banister, crying in pain and total frustration. George smiled knowingly and ran off to fetch me the wheelchair that he had already signed out for my use. The staff at Headley are simply the best. George's challenge made a huge impact on me and was definitely the turning point in my attitude, as I needed to listen to their advice and then act upon it. After concluding my stay at Headley, I was taken to Selly Oak for a routine hospital appointment.

8 Mar 07

At my routine appointment I explained that I was unable to continue with therapy at Headley Court due to the infection (slough) continually oozing out of my toes after sustaining any pressure. As I had got to know the nurses in out patients, they let me take my own bandages off my thumbs and toes. It was while taking off my left toes bandage that I felt something give inside the sopping wet infected dressing. As I quietly cringed in pain, I gently pulled the dressing away from my yucky skin, then I realised that the made up toe from my pelvis had actually come away. I was left with bits of rotten skin and part of a bone just looking at me. I know I had wound up the nurses previously with some of my jokes, but this one was going to take the biscuit. A civilian nurse named Jo came into my cubicle and burst out laughing thinking it was some kind of prank, seconds later came the look of horror as she saw it dripping with slough. After the Dr's examined both my toes, they requested that I returned to Selly Oak on Mon 12 Mar to have both toes debrided and skin grafted again. During that weekend in reaction to all the appalling press coverage that Selly Oak hospital had received from a few dis-satisfied military patients, I wrote a letter to the Royal Air Force News, expressing how well I had been treated by all members of staff in particular the nurses and welfare staff. I guess all patients review places in context as to how they were treated. Then again, I felt that some gullible patients had just jumped on the band wagon, but I for one was overwhelmed with Selly Oaks support and believe they achieve an outstanding job.

12 Mar 07

Today came around all too quickly, at 0700 hours a driver from RAF High Wycombe arrived outside the house and took me to Selly Oak for my out patients appointment. I had an amusing time with the staff, followed by being wheeled down to theatre to meet up with the surgeon and anaesthetist team. This was my 4th operation in 3 months, so I knew the routine. The only difference this time, I tried telling a joke while being administered my anaesthetic to see if when I woke up, could I come out with the punch line.

The operation took 90 minutes which successfully debrided my left toe, they then took a skin graft from my right thigh to seal things up. Although waking up groggy, I gave them the punch line much to the amusement of the team. Within 3 hours I was back in the car, being driven back to Faringdon.

13 Mar - 15 Apr 07
Back at home my medical support was once again being provided by RAF Brize Norton. Using specially devised crutches, which required no use of my thumbs, my walking progressed daily and my toes slowly started to heal. I think my attitude also helped as no longer was I trying to ignore the extent of my injuries. While at home the floods of emails and phone calls continued, which included the heads up that the RAF were establishing a Unit Enquiry, to find out how I and Pita had sustained frostbite. The RAF wanted various questions answering to see who the finger could be pointed at or was it just a freak of nature. Once established I believe that the whole report should have been concluded within 3 months and then forwarded to an RAF executive for their recommendations. Just as I thought things had taken a turn for the better with my attitude, the creation of this enquiry seemed to be the start of yet another roller coaster ride giving me both good and bad news.

16 - 26 Apr 07
Today I started my second visit to Headley Court, this time it was heaps better. With the use of my adapted crutches the remedial instructors and occupational health teams managed to increase my walking up to ½ a mile, without me suffering too much pain. The physiotherapists could actually manipulate both my toes and work on the desensitisation of my thumbs; this was exactly what I needed. Over a period of only 2 weeks, I was almost independent but most importantly, I was now fit enough to drive, having so much more flexibility in my feet. Before actually sitting behind the wheel, I visited Selly Oak and spoke to a pain specialist who revised my medication, which had now been reduced from 42 tablets a day in February and March, down to 12 tablets and the tick in the box to drive. Also during my stay in Headley, the president of the Unit Enquiry turned up and started to question me about my side of the events. I personally found this amusing. As his first question was *"why do you think, you go frostbite?"* to which I replied *"because it was f*&king cold, are you taking the pi**?"* Fortunately my doctor got word that this guy was in the building,

following which he was politely asked to leave, so I may continue with my recovery. I was happy to talk to him as I wanted the truth to come out about Pita's mistake!

27 Apr - 7 May 07

With my new independence, Clare and I drove up with Joshua to see Kieran in Inverness for an extended weekend. We also visited the guys from the RAF Mountain Rescue Service and our friends who had been so supportive to both Clare and I over the past 6 months. Kieran was on top form, loving the time with his baby brother and trying to explain to him the importance of supporting Rangers and Manchester United. As I'm a lifelong Liverpool fan, the last 6 months had also been life changing for him as when I left he was supporting Celtic and Liverpool, that will teach me to go away. How much more pain could I take?

8 May 07

Having 7 months off, was something that I had obviously never experienced, as before December 2006, I had totalled only 7 days off sick in 24 years, something that I was very proud of. With that record out of the window, today I went back to work. With all my weight loss, my uniform hung off me, which seemed insignificant as most of the attention would be on my open sandals and heavily bandaged thumbs. As I entered the building, walking up the stairs independently I started my smile, but the reception from my friends and colleagues was overwhelming. No sooner did I walk into the office, I was greeted with the command that it was about time I'd made it into work as it was my turn to make the tea. Just sitting around RAF troops in uniform, listening to their banter and the whinges about the management was like time stood still, as this is exactly what I had left behind in October; it was fantastic. I spent the majority of the day, just catching up with friends, repeating the same story time and time again, but I was back. The ironic point of today was I had to book an appointment with the doctor, as officially I was still on sick leave. The doctor took a lot of convincing that I was fit for work, but considering I'd previously raised just over £180K for the expedition, convincing him was one of my easier tasks I had undertaken over the past few months. The first few weeks past quite slowly as I was incredibly tired, with the driving to and from work and the fact I was actively using my brain again. I was immensely frustrated even to the point of tears as to why my memory was so poor but bearing in mind the copious amount of drugs I had taken since January, this soon made sense. Throughout this entire episode, Clare had taken all of life's punches on the chin for both of us and was showing the obvious signs of exhaustion. So with me picking up a routine within work and home gave us both a refreshing new start and a breath of fresh air.

24 May 07

Today I visited Selly Oak for a routine appointment, which concluded that the infection within my toes was reducing and at long last they were starting to heal over. As per all out patient appointments, I reported to the military administration office only to be asked if I was prepared to be included within a survey of military patients who had been treated within Selly Oak over the past year. Having been so impressed with my treatment I happily accepted the interview and went on to highly commend everyone for their exceptional help during my treatment, I further went onto emphasise that I probably couldn't have been treated as well if I had returned from Antarctica as a civilian.

31 May 07

Over the past month, even though I'm progressing and had returned to work I've found that I'm very low and feel depressed about any issue that maybe presented to me; I seem to find a very negative approach to everything. I've sat down with Clare and we've decided to get some advice from a doctor and possibly speak to a psychiatric nurse. After various discussions I was finally introduced to the mental health team at Brize Norton, who specialise in this field. In a nutshell over the past 24 years of serving with the Mountain Rescue Service and then heading straight into organising the South Pole, I've never really allowed any of the numerous traumas that I have witnessed, to be digested within my mind. Having so much time on my hands so far this year, has allowed a tsunami of memories and emotions time to catch up and bite me in the bum. This with the great frustration of not being able to get back into any form of normal living with my injuries was just the cherry on top. My first meeting opened up an abyss of disaster. The clinical practise nurse Corporal Rob Morris, casually asked me to list on the magic board what thoughts and emotions were currently going around my mind. On taking the pen, I listed 3 columns adding up to 27 events. He sat there dumbfounded, he was expecting around 4 or 5 maybe 6. So calmly Rob explains that we can address each of these issues 1 at a time, but before our next meeting, could I try and prioritise them. As I sat in my car before driving home, I felt mixed emotions as I had actually shared my uttermost thoughts with a stranger, but I had also realised that I was carrying so much baggage in one tiny head. Without warning, I burst into tears, this was going to hurt.

12 Jun 07

Today I met the RAF's Occupational Health co-ordinator based at RAF Lyneham. What he wanted to assess was, am I physically capable of fulfilling my primary task as a communicator? Having only seen the psychiatric nurse a day or so earlier, I really didn't care too much about the outcome of this meeting, until the 1000 lb mortar bomb was dropped. The assessor predicted that I should make a good enough recovery for me to continue working within the RAF but my operational tours and adventurous training days are over. In other words, I'm fit for purpose but I would be forbidden to serve in Iraq, Afghanistan, Falkland Islands or go climbing or walking while on duty. I cannot emphasise enough that the RAF has been my life for over 24 years, so his comments can only be compared to having the hardest kick in your testicles you could ever imagine. Realistically once our conversation had concluded, I just wanted to leave the RAF as in my opinion, I had nothing to offer. I am a man of pride, how the hell could I lead a section of troops, and send one of the guys overseas to an area of conflict, when I couldn't operate there myself? One good aspect that came from the meeting was the assessor made a special recommendation that I visit a frostbite injury specialist at the Institute of Naval Medicine at Gosport. His description of this chap was very intriguing so I eagerly pushed for a referral, which the assessor thankfully processed for me immediately. As I was in the Lyneham area, I seized the opportunity to visit a great friend of mine Pete Ross, another RAF mountain rescue hero from the 1980's who stuck the kettle on. Roscoe is an inspirational character who doesn't know the meaning of the word "no", so he was the perfect guy to speak to after receiving such crap news. He suggested that I totally ignored the recommendations of the bloke and what is more important is to get my fitness back so we can go out climbing again. Unfortunately Roscoe's enthusiasm didn't remain in my mind very long. As while driving home back to Clare the implications and reality of no more operations or adventurous training really hit me. This chapter all seemed to becoming a little more serious than just losing the ends of my thumbs and toes.

19 Jun 07

As promised the occupational health assessor had immediately processed my referral to meet Dr Howard Oakley, a leading expert on frostbite and non freeze injuries. So as Clare had a day off, we enjoyed a quick drive down to the South coast. Clare went off to meet one of her retired police colleagues as I met this incredible character, whom had previously worked on Antarctica and had over 20 years of treating military personnel who had suffered from some kind of cold injury. After a very friendly reception we sat both sat back while I explained everything that had happened over the past 6 months. Being the enthusiastic character that I am, I energetically went on for over an hour so everything that you've read so far about my outstanding treatment, the ground breaking surgery, and the incredible efforts made at Headley Court and so on, were relayed to him. It wasn't until I stopped that I realised Dr Oakley had been taking lots of notes and still hadn't ask me any questions, as I thought I was leaving no stone unturned with my detail.

What was about to happen in the next 10 minutes would change my life forever. After eventually concluding my story, Dr Oakley very calmly asked a question. *"Had I ever heard or read the Joint Service Publication 539?"* My answer was clearly no. A Joint Service Publication (JSP) is a United Kingdom Ministry of Defence related document. A JSP is an authoritative set of rules or guidelines with defence-wide applicability or interest. Many are connected with safety or engineering or health and, as such, are considered important documents for those working in those areas. Howard pressed a few buttons on his computer and printed off several pages from the JSP 539 entitled "Heat illness and Cold injury – Prevention and Management". The first page stated that no injury sustaining frostbite should undergo surgery for a minimum of 6 months, the second page stated that no transplantation should take place for a minimum of 14 months.

My heart dropped like a 16 lb sledge hammer hitting your foot. I looked up at him and wanted to ask a question, I physically couldn't, instead the tears rolled down my face. What the hell had happened to me? I then had an urge of wanting to projectile vomit. In those split seconds my world had stopped, what energy had been recharged, what smile had started to appear had been napalmed. The silence was broken by Dr Oakley, who phoned his secretary asking her to kindly bring through 2 mugs of sweet tea. Over the next few moments Dr Oakley moved from behind his table and squeezed his hand on my sunken shoulder and quietly said, this is why you have been referred to me, I will help you rebuild yourself. While drinking our brew, he went on to explain the several options I had, all of which concluded with the same answer; there were definitely no overseas operations or adventurous training.

The only thought I could muster was throughout the whole of the period 29 Dec 06 – 07 Jan 07, I was visited by an abundance of military medical staff, who due to the unique injuries were very interested to not only see my injuries but to hear how it had happened. At no stage did anyone ever mention the JSP 539 which had been released Dec 06 and obviously no one had prevented my unlawful transplant operation. Dr Oakley then suggested that I phoned Clare, so he could meet her and explain about the Armageddon situation that I had now experienced. The look on Clare's face as Dr Oakley enlightened her on what should have happened was horrifying, as it was not only me who had been through the past 6 months of turmoil. Up to 90 mins ago, I had been enthusiastically promoting what treatment I had received; now my world had fallen apart. Before leaving, Dr Oakley advised us about the Armed Forces Compensation Scheme (AFCS) and details of an organisation that assists people who struggle with post frostbite injuries. This would not be the last time I would meet Dr Oakley as over the next few months I would undertake various tests. Here his team would submerge my hands and feet in cold water at a specific temperature and time and then monitor them with a thermal imaging device to assess how quickly the heat returned. The process called thermology discovered over a period of a year, that the heat returned quicker in some areas than others but noticeably my thumb stumps always remained cold regardless of time or heat exchanged.

Over the coming weeks, Clare and I discussed at length what options we should take with regards to the AFCS and finding a solicitor to review the surgery I had undergone; this was to be the start of 3 years of upset and more mayhem.

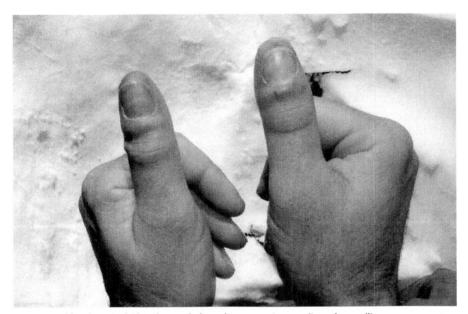

First signs of frostbite. Both thumbs needed regular puncturing to relieve the swelling.

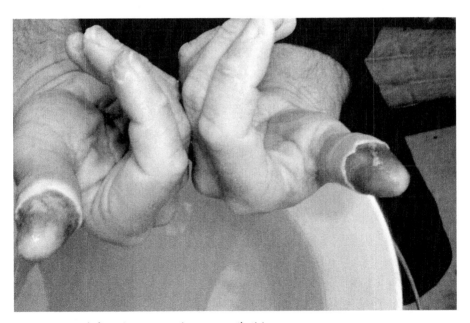

Damage exposed after mior surgery using no anaesthetic!

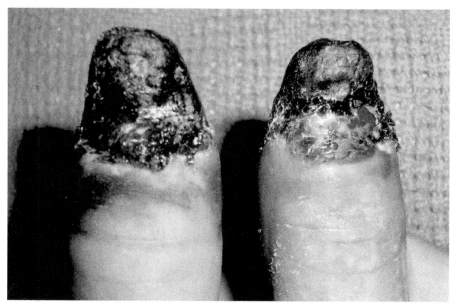

Back at Selly Oak in Birmingham, the thumbs are showing classice signs of frostbite. Note I've already knocked the tip of my right thumb.

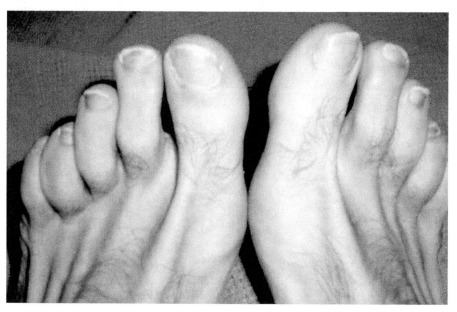

A picture to authenticate there was nothing wrong with my feet when I first returned!

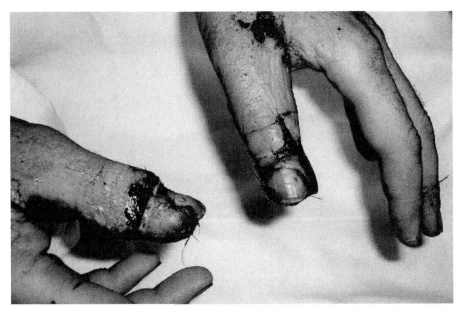

Unbelievable! My toes have been transplanted onto my thumbs...

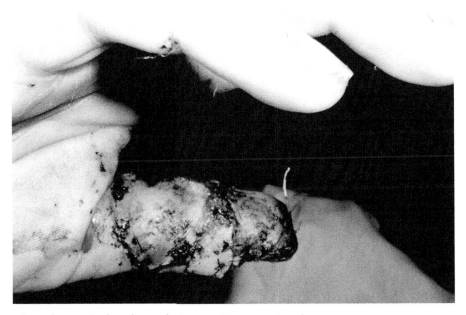

... but unfortunately after a few weeks the transplants were rejected.

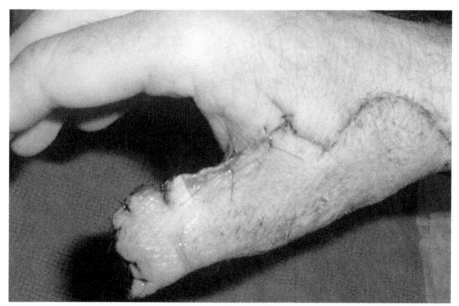

The next time you have a chicken wing on the BBQ, try not to think about this photo!

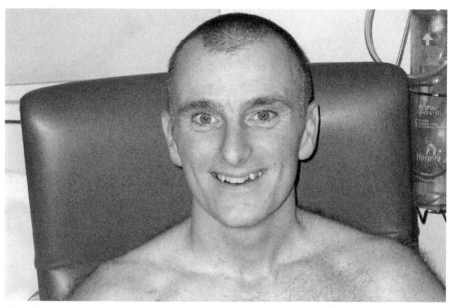

Still smiling, but the effects of over six weeks on Antarctica and three weeks in hospital on antibiotics are clear to see.

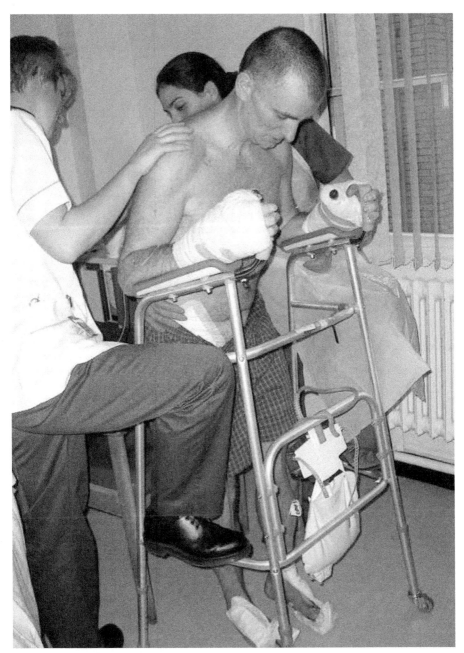

I will be forever grateful to both ladies for getting me walking again. I'm still catheterised and connected to a morphine pump.

Sir Brian Burridge, myself and Sir Joe French at the welcome home reception.

Chapter 10
Depression

As mentioned on 31 May 07, I touched base with a clinical practise nurse Rob Morris who had been taken back a gasp by the volume of thoughts I routinely had spinning around my mind. Throughout the whole of my 24 years in the RAF I have always been a determined and enthusiastic troop who had never really envisaged or accepted any failure throughout my career. I had been promoted ahead of my peers, I had been awarded an MBE, I had maintained an extremely high level of fitness and had been selected by the RAF's MRS to lead two of their teams at RAF Leeming and RAF Kinloss, both of these positions are viewed by most as being the highest accolades within the MRS. When presented with a challenge, I had always given my upmost effort for it to succeed regardless of size or proportion. Over the past 6 months my body had been beaten into submission of amputation and within the past 3 weeks, I had been psychologically battered. It felt like a gigantic sized door which led to failure had opened and was vacuuming me towards it on another blue ice runway.

Following my first appointment, Rob had sourced permission for me to visit him weekly at Brize Norton as the volume of trauma that I had written on the magic board had raised many concerns. I had as requested tried to prioritise my list of thoughts and over the coming months Rob and I shared my upmost secret anxieties and fears while trying to maintain a normal work live balance. Some of the thoughts dissipated naturally as we proved there was nothing neither he nor I could do to change the situation. For example the loss of my father, who died of cancer at the age of 61 when I was only 18 years old. I had resented his loss for so many years as I listened to fellow troops preaching how their parents were no longer important to them. That was their thoughts; I could treasure my wonderful memories rather than begrudge the thoughts of others. The opening of all these ragged cardboard boxes within my mind, started to take their strain, so Rob asked me to consider taking an antidepressant tablet called Citalopram. My initial response was pure resentment towards him. I was seething as the stigma and the embarrassment of taking medication simply added up to more failure. Rob was the epitome of a polite punch bag; he so calmly took my comments on the chin and then delicately served them back to me. I knew in my sinking heart of hearts he was right, I trusted him impeccably but I secretly hoped that he would back down and say, we'll carry on without them, but he didn't. The gigantic door of failure had opened even further. As we progressed through my list, we came across incidents that talking about or even writing an account couldn't repair or even slightly close the tattered cardboard box within my head. On one occasion, I explained how I had been the co-ordinator of a search for a missing aircraft in Scotland that took over 3 months to find. The aircraft was eventually located by a couple of climbers who had approached the mountain by an unclimbed gully and had innocently come across a life raft and wreckage. The mental punishment and guilt I had put myself through during the 3 months was topped off by me insisting that I recovered the crew.

My thoughts of the recovery had been very clouded until Rob tried a relatively new technique called Eye Movement Desensitization and Reprocessing (EMDR). EMDR is a psychotherapy treatment that was designed to alleviate the distress associated with traumatic memories. Rob administered EMDR on me, which over a period of an hour had opened up my memory to remember a full account of the recovery. Even though it brought back harrowing memories, the fact that I could now account for all my actions allowed me to slowly close the lid on that specific box.

As we approached the end of 2007, I was given dates for my final rehabilitation course at Headley Court. So immediately after the festive period I drove to Headley where I started another intense course of rehab on my feet and hands. By the end of the first week I had proved that I had been following their guidance as I was physically fit as a butcher's dog. As I came home on the Friday, I felt emotionally shell shocked as now I had proved to the consultants I was physically OK, but mentally, I was a still sliding into a huge black hole.

As Clare left for work on Sunday morning, I felt uneasy and void of virtually all my emotions, like I was running on empty. After lunch I remember, putting Joshua into his rear car seat and driving into the nearby countryside trying to spark some reaction into me or to find freedom of some kind, there was nothing. With my heart racing and in an almost slow motion panic, I drove around 15 miles to a layby that's situated just behind the Police Headquarters, where I knew Clare was working. With Joshua now asleep, I stepped out of my car and just wanted to walk off and disappear. I remember holding my head in my hands and crying uncontrollably as I crouched down hidden by the car on the inside of the layby. I must have been there an hour before fighting with my feelings to force myself to drive home. I must have put Joshua in his cot with a bottle of milk as that is where Clare found him crying when she came home. As Clare came downstairs, she found me on the floor huddled up behind the back of the 3 seater settee and the living room wall, I was completely broken. Clare tells me that over a period of time she carefully coerced me to come out from behind the settee to sit in the chair. I just continued to cry while repeating that I'm sorry, I'm sorry, I'm sorry. Clare made various calls to the National Health Service mental health teams, but as no one was in immediate danger, there was nothing they could do. She then phoned the guardroom at RAF Brize Norton trying to get hold of Rob Morris.

Clare received a call back from an RAF police officer who offered to come and remove me from the house in the interest of safety for Joshua and her. Clare politely advised the guy that she was a civilian police officer and that would not be necessary. I believe over the next couple of hours Clare sat holding me while reassuring me that I was going to be alright. One of the first things I do remember as I came out of this dense fog experience was when our clock chimed 2100 hours, I thought the mountain rescue teams will now be back safely after their weekend's training. The past 5 or 6 hours had been dissolved from my memory, but thankfully Joshua, Clare and I were safe. Within minutes of the fog clearing and me returning to reality, I felt exhausted and fell asleep.

That night I should have driven back to Headley Court for my second week of rehab, but as I was exhausted, I drove back on Monday morning. As I arrived at Headley I tried to hide what had happened last night, but during my first chat with one of the physical training instructors, I broke down in tears and spilled the lot. He immediately introduced me to Headley's clinical practise nurse, who rekindled my repair process once again following a lengthy conversation with Rob at Brize Norton.

On completion of my rehab at Headley, Rob broke the news to me that he was posted and would be handing over my care to Corporal Rachel Banks. He also suggested that following my incident at home, I should increase my Citalopram to 40 mgs. Meeting Rachel was at first a very testing period, as having previously opened my heart and soul to Rob, I was having to repeat the painful process. Rachel was amazing and within weeks had built my complete trust so I may continue my repairing process. She introduced me to a book called Mind Over Mood, containing exercises in cognitive behaviour therapy. At first, I cynically mistreated the books intentions as I felt the exercises were all very patronising. However with Rachel's patient perseverance and after several failed attempts, the exercises started to help.

I remained under the guidance of Rachel for almost 2 years, during which I tried to come off the medication but with the emotions that I started to display again, it was obvious that I should retake them and remain in my bubble. I say bubble as that is how Citalopram made me feel. At 40 mgs, I could see the shape of someone touching my bubble from outside, although I could not feel any physical contact. At 30 mgs, the indentation of my bubble being prodded was a lot more visible and this time I could feel a slight sensation of being touched, but still I was protected from any hard physical contact. At 20 mgs, the amount at which I took for the majority of my treatment, I could actually feel some form of physical contact but knowing I had taken my Citalopram this morning, I knew I was safe. 10 mgs, was like a trial of how much reality I could take in a day. This time your bubble is virtually invisible as you feel every blow, it's simply down to you to utilise your mind exercises to help you handle the situation.

There are various antidepressants available all prescribed via a doctor, I was fortunate that Citalopram worked for me. I fully understand that depression differs in so many variations with every person who suffers from it, but depression is relative to that individual. How both Rob and Rachel came to their conclusions on how to treat me can only be described as a gift. I owe them both so much and it would not be an overstatement, to say, they saved my life. Although like you I still have my down days, I now hold various keys that can help me let the depressing thoughts subside before they take over my daily mood. The golden key is admitting you need help and then seek it. Your aspirations, your anxieties, your life will change once you've made that call to book an appointment, if I can do it, what is stopping you?

May 2008

After enduring months of pain, I decided to have another operation to remove some extremely painful nerves from my left thumb and foot. As I was admitted a couple of days in advance of my operation to allow the surgeon time to assess me, I persuaded him to arrange for me to have a vasectomy while under the same general anaesthetic. All 3 elements of the operation went to plan but this would be the last time I would visit Selly Oak, as during my stay, I relived the painful realisation that I should not have undergone any surgery at all.

As I recovered from the operation and in light I was soon to complete my tour of duty with the COMSEC team, I enquired to see what positions were available to me, as with all my restrictions, I was planning on leaving the RAF. I met Sergeant Jayne Williams who had the overall picture of available positions in and out of trade. I told her that I had virtually nothing to offer, as the RAF would not authorise me to serve on operations and the thought of doing an office job was a nonstarter. My conversation with Jayne gave me something to chew on over the next few weeks as she was suggesting that I applied for the position as the Warrant Officer on the Air Member for Personnel's briefing team. If accepted, this job working alongside 2 senior Officers would provide the personnel working at the RAF's coal face the opportunity to ask questions which would be fed back to the 2nd in command of the RAF. I immediately sparked at the idea, that if I couldn't join the troops at the front line, I could at least support them in any way I could, while representing one the RAF's highest executive officers.

The job over the next 3 years saw me travel on average 75000 miles a year, visiting 66 stations, presenting to 1000's of RAF personnel in locations around the world. Whether talking to the youngest, junior member of the station or the senior Warrant Officer, if they presented me a substantiated complaint or recommendation, I gave them my word that they would receive a response within a month. Although again I had to sacrifice my time at home with Clare and Joshua in Faringdon, I also somehow maintained my monthly visits to see Kieran in Inverness. Most importantly, this position gave me a purpose and reignited my enthusiasm to aspire others.

Within my 3 years on the road, the wheels of my Armed Forces Compensation Scheme and my claim against the surgeon came to fruition, as I accepted an out of court settlement. Ironically the payment co-insided with the release of the findings of the Unit Enquiry, which had taken over 22 months to conclude. Remembering this should have taken approximately 12 weeks, by now I felt the whole proceeding was a farce. Not only that, I had had the whole worry of the enquiry over my head while struggling with depression. When I was ordered (not invited) to attend, the conclusions were read out to me by an executive officer; I honestly didn't know whether to laugh or cry. The President of the Board was a commissioned Air Traffic Controller, the subject matter expert was a physical training instructor with little or no cold weather experience and the findings/conclusions were virtually all taken from my personal diary.

When I was told that I was to blame for Pita's frostbite, I gracefully smiled and disrespectfully suggested that she better get herself a bloody good solicitor. Looking back that was definitely the better of the 2 options that I quickly processed in my mind as the 2nd option would have meant spending time at Her Majesty's pleasure behind bars. 22 months to be told that I should have checked his clothing was pathetic. I was the Expedition Leader and had provided him every stitch of clothing; should I after 2½ of training have had to dress him too? Ironically after losing so much sleep and being stressed by the unknown conclusions for so long, I felt the board's findings would be better served feeding my newly planted potato crop, as it was full of manure. Strangely enough after walking out with a smile and spring in my step, I never heard another thing.

While on the road with the team, although I constantly wore gloves to encourage the blood to reach my extremities, I continually suffered with poor circulation and very cold hands. So while back at High Wycombe in May 2009, I enquired if I may receive treatment at another hospital rather than

Selly Oak. Within days I was invited to meet a hand surgeon at the Royal Free Hospital in London. With details of my previous operations, I proceeded to explain what treatment I had received, to which he was almost speechless. He examined my thumbs and toes and suggested that although most of the skin had been utilised to cover up previous operations, he was confident, he could improve my circulation and divert a nerve from my wedding ring finger to the left thumb stump to give me some form of sensation. The following month I reported to the Royal Free where he carried micro surgery on my left hand. Within a month the results were superb and for the first time, I now had some sensation in my left thumb, which didn't resemble pain.

August 2011

My 3 years on the road came to an end when I was invited to choose a posting of my choice. With several options on the table, I chose a Joint Service position as the College Warrant Officer (CWO) at the Joint Services Command and Staff College at the Defence Academy, Shrivenham only 5 miles away from Faringdon. At long last after all the time I had spent away from home, I could now start to repay Clare and spend more time with Joshua.

As CWO I worked within a team of people who co-ordinated the training of the United Kingdom's Armed Forces Commissioned Officers. We would routinely have around 500 Officers each week, attending courses varying from 1 week to 9 months long. It was brilliant and with such a great team, the college worked like clockwork.

April 2012

With my fitness and health improving, I discreetly decided to start piecing together an expedition to trek to Mount Everest Base Camp (EBC). Knowing that the military wouldn't authorise me to go, I put a leave pass in for 3 weeks for April 2012. It took me around 9 months to put a team together of great friends and family which included both military and civilian troops. As this was a civilian trip, I had no red tape to wade through and no financial worries.

It was brilliant and it turned out to be one of my favourite expeditions I've ever been on, even if I say so myself. From the moment your eyes opened until your eyes shut, the team constantly supported each other, the team took the mickey out of each other but most of all we all tasted freedom from the RAF. With the temperature of around -15 degrees and to the contrary of the RAF findings, I happily managed my thumbs and toes, the only thing I couldn't stop was the tears of joy freezing to my face as I finally summited Kala Pattar at a height of 5555 metres. I had summited before in 2003 but seeing the breath taking view of the mother goddess of mountains, Mount Everest again after all that had happened in the past 6 years made the moment even more special. The cherry on top was to share a photo with my brother Ian, the boys from Grimsby had done well. I was back in the mountains where I belong and the RAF couldn't stop me.

Returning from Mt Everest was a huge turning point in my life. My first day back after the expedition was not as the CWO, as I had planned a medical appointment at RAF Henlow, the organisation that could upgrade my medical status. After being examined by 2 independent doctors, they concluded that I was still not eligible to serve overseas, as in their opinion my thumbs and toes were too sensitive to the various temperatures. As I listened to his conclusions, I broke his trail of discussion by highlighting that less than 10 days ago I had ascended Kala Pattar. Regardless of my claim, his conclusions remained the same as he advised me that the RAF had a duty of care to look after their personnel regardless of the individuals aspirations. I reluctantly but respectfully understood, but I knew as I signed the form to acknowledge his recommendations, it was the beginning of the end of my RAF career.

On returning home, Clare and I discussed my various options but as I knew my next position would be within an office in London, my mind was made up. So together we pencilled a plan together for me to leave the RAF in October 2014.

With so much time on my hands, I started to provide more inspirational presentations on the South Pole expedition to various organisations including schools, colleges and universities. I just wanted to inspire our future generation to follow their dreams. This gave me an idea as to which direction I should take starting in 2015. First of all, with a little over a year to go, I decided I wanted to finish my final 6 weeks in the RAF with one final challenge, but to achieve it would mean undergoing one more operation. I knew if I followed the standard military procedures, it would be a none starter, so I approached the Royal Free hospital surgeon directly enquiring was it possible to open the web between my thumb and first finger on my left hand and could he remove another annoying nerve in my left foot. When I explained that I wanted to walk unsupported between Land's End and John O'Groats in memory of my best mate, he sarcastically burst out laughing and asked when did I want the operation? I then approached the medical centre at Shrivenham, explaining that I was suffering with excessive pain in my left foot and I was struggling with the restricted use of my left hand. Thankfully the guys arranged the appointments and I had surgery within 6 weeks. I knew this was a self inflicted operation but it meant before leaving the RAF, I could once again use walking poles and wear sturdy mountaineering boots. Once again the surgeon was brilliant; he removed all the pain from my left foot and gave me around 75% usage of my left hand.

My final year in the RAF was primarily spent working through a diploma in supporting teachers so that I may follow my aspiration to teach children with special educational needs. As the Royal Air Force had given me so many opportunities over 31 years, I feel it was a fitting tribute and time for me to pay something back to the future of our country. After months of painful training, I utilised my last 6 weeks of Service by completing the 881 miles unsupported walk in memory of my best friend Dean Singleton raising over £24K for the Hospice that let him die with so much dignity.

Chapter 11
Conclusion

It has taken me 3 attempts to complete this book. The first 2 attempts ended prematurely as I started to remind myself of some of the horrific events that I had endured over the period. Some of which were simply far too difficult to contend with, especially when suffering from depression. Even this time, it's induced many tears and steered up memories that are probably best forgotten. But as all the details are now contained in one area, maybe I will find completion at last. I just hope that this can inspire you to follow your dreams. I conclude all my presentations with 2 comments. Firstly, I have no regrets, I have stood at the South Pole and no one can take that away from me. Secondly every single person has an aspiration of varying degrees; the only person stopping them achieving that aspiration looks them in the mirror every time they clean their teeth. It's you, so if you have that reoccurring dream, follow it, I mean what could go wrong?

I could not conclude this book without a word about my 2 adopted brothers Iain Kirk and Phil Mainprize. All 3 of us have experienced similar emotions that can only be compared to that of grief or the loss of losing someone or something. I've learnt that the five effects of grief are described as denial and isolation, anger, bargaining, depression and finally acceptance. The 3 of us have approached and processed the effects in our own personal way. What I've written in this book has only scratched the surface of what we shared while on the ice together and what we've experienced since returning, but the bond and strength of our friendship has proven to be unbreakable. I am so proud and honoured to have shared Antarctica with them and the memories that we created will be treasured until my grave. Although we live miles apart we utilise the excuse of meeting up each year to rotate the ownership of the picture that MSgt Ken Howk and his 56th RQS team presented to us. That reminds me Phil, it's my turn! Oh and finally, thanks again for letting me use the Sat phone at the Pole, you are and always will be part of Clare and my life, we love you guys.

So many people have helped me over the years and I feel it would be wrong of me to name them all, but one person has stuck with me every second of the way. When Clare first met me at Dean Singleton's house in 2004, one of the things that attracted her to me was my drive and passion towards my dream of reaching the South Pole. Since then Clare has witnessed the very best in me and undoubtedly the worst, but has stayed by my side throughout. Before marrying in March 2009, Clare had painfully watched me slowly change from the inspiring, determined and positive individual to a bubbling wreck squeezed between our 3 seater settee and the wall. Over the years Clare has been my impregnable rock, her endless love and support while I have displayed moments of anger and frustration has been incredible. I can honestly say I couldn't have done any of this without her. Clare Sylvester-Wyness is my soulmate who I did go to the end of the earth for and would, without hesitation do it again, if only she would let me...

Acknowledgements

Phil Mainprize and Iain Kirk your photographs are phenomenal.

To all the people who visited me while in Selly Oak hospital and for the amazing support you gave Clare throughout my stay, thank you from the bottom of my heart.

On behalf of the expedition, a very large and sincere thank you is owed to the following for helping to allow the expedition to take place:

HRH The Duke of Edinburgh, Sir Brian Burridge, Sir Joe French, Station Commanders RAF's High Wycombe, Halton, Kinloss, Leuchars, the Inspector of Recruiting at Cranwell, Squadron Leader (Retired) Kev Eaton, Tom Taylor at the Mission Control Centre RAF Kinloss, Rob Morris, Rachel Banks, Chilean Air Force, Mike Sharp and his team from ALE, David Stock FCO, Petty Officer Rook British Embassy Santiago; Physical Education Flight, Service Funds and Accounts staff at RAF High Wycombe; Warrant Officer Steve Metcalfe; RAF Central Service Funds; Defence Storage and Distribution Centre Bicester, Gary Hoyland at the RAF Sports Lottery, Chris Toms, David Hempleman-Adams, Zoe Hudson, Sjur Mordre, Ken Howk and the members of USAF 56 RQS, Babcock Defence Services, QINETIQ, SYSIS, Austin Hayes, ESS, First Choice Expedition Foods, HR Smith, Havelock School Grimsby, Edward Heneage School Grimsby, Lady Getty, Mr & Mrs John Emberson, David Emberson.

Please accept an even sincere apology if I have not included your name, I'm sure I must owe you a beer or two.

Biography

Al Sylvester grew up in Grimsby, North East Lincolnshire. There, with great encouragement from his family, he shared a wonderful childhood with his mother, father and 2 brothers and sister, enjoying his education and also serving within the Scouting Association, which concluded with being awarded the Chief Scouts Award.

Within a year of joining the Royal Air Force as a Communicator in 1983, Al volunteered for the RAF Mountain Rescue Service (MRS) where he served on various teams, attending over 350 rescue operations throughout his 21 years. During his time as Team Leader of RAF Leeming MRS Al was awarded an MBE for services to the mountain rescue and for supporting the Imperial Cancer Research Fund by helping, with his team to raise over £350,000.

Following an Operational tour in Croatia/Bosnia in 1998, Al was promoted to Team Leader at RAF Kinloss MRS, where during his 3 years tenure; he led the RAF MRS first combat overseas response to an RAF Hercules aircraft crash in Kukes, Albania. He also led the search and recovery of two United States Air Force F15 fast jets from the Cairngorms, Scotland which concluded as one of the largest military aircraft crash operations in the RAF MRS history.
On promotion to Warrant Officer, Al retired from the MRS and fulfilled a communication security post at the RAF's Headquarters Air Command at High Wycombe. During this time, he followed his lifelong ambition to lead the RAF's first unsupported expedition to the Geographic South Pole. His four man team were forced to abort their attempt after completing 509 nautical miles and only five days from the Pole due to a life threatening injury sustained by one of his team.

Following the polar expedition Al was selected for the role of Air Member for Personnel's Warrant Officer, where as a three person team, visited 66 military units housing the 42000 RAF personnel around the world per year, presenting current and future policy. His RAF career concluded at the Defence Academy of the UK based at Shrivenham, near Swindon, Wiltshire. As the Warrant Officer, he maintained the discipline and deportment of over 450 military Officers whilst ensuring that each VIP visitor would be hosted to the highest standard within one of the finest military colleges in the world. In recognition of his outstanding service, Al was awarded the Meritorious Service Medal.

On retirement from the RAF, Al has settled in Oxfordshire, in the market town of Faringdon, where he works within the Faringdon Academy of Schools as a special educational needs teaching assistant.

Other publications

Walk to Freedom is a brutally honest account of Al's unsupported 881 mile, 40 day walk between Land's End and John O'Groats. It also describes his walk from the RAF into civvy street and back to the Highlands where he spent his most memorable times with his best friend Dean Singleton while serving in the RAF Mountain Rescue Service. Read how Al overcomes the physical and mental evils involved with walking on the UK's roads, evading the treacherous oncoming traffic of some of this country's worst drivers!

Exercise - Everest Dreams provides a breathtaking view through the eye of the camera of the stunning views you witness while trekking into Mount Everest's base camp at over 18000 ft. It also includes Al's personal diary, detailing the route, the height gained and the emotions felt as you trek to one of the world's highest campsites. *"The Himalaya's will bring tears to your eyes and then gently freeze them to your face."*

If you would like further details on either book, or about Al's future motivational presentations, he can be contacted by email at **alsylvester@yahoo.co.uk**

Printed in Great Britain
by Amazon

41779484R00121